"This book is more than a page-turner. It's a game-changer. It's courageous. It's bold. It's vulnerable and funny and redemptive. It's a revolutionary way to see suffering, which Jesus modeled two thousand years ago. You will learn that no one is exempt from difficulty. We don't get a pass when it comes to pain. But we can worship God in our weakness because pain has a way of clearing out the clutter in our lives. It burns off the excess and allows us to see what really matters after all: the people we love, the message we carry, and the God we worship."

From the foreword by **Mark Batterson**, author of *The Grave Robber*

"What a rare and beautiful gift it is for a man to fully open his broken heart. My friend Clayton does just that in this book. He helped me see God isn't breaking me but actually making me. You will gain such needed perspective and comfort from these pages."

Lysa TerKeurst, president, Proverbs 31 Ministries; *New York Times* bestselling author of *The Best Yes*

"Clayton is one of the most gifted gospel communicators I've ever known—one of my preaching heroes. But this book is not a message, it is the revelation of his soul. Clayton is a man who has walked through fire, a fire God used to forge him into an instrument of grace. This book will not inspire you. It will transform you."

J. D. Greear, PhD, author of *Jesus, Continued . . . Why the Spirit Inside You Is Better than Jesus Beside You* and *Gospel: Recovering the Power That Made Christianity Revolutionary*

"I've known Clayton since we were teenagers. He's not only one of the greatest communicators I've ever heard speak but also one of the best friends I've ever had. I watched him go through the valley of the shadow of death over the course of a dozen years and I was blown away by how he remained open to the Holy Spirit throughout that hard season. His transparency is disarming and refreshing, something the church desperately needs from its leaders. He has blessed me as a friend and has blessed NewSpring Church as a pastor and leader who is not afraid to be real and authentic. In *Stronger*, he speaks with authority because he's lived through tragedy and loss, and he speaks with tenderness because his experience has helped him relate to all of us who have known pain, doubt, and fear. Clayton shows us how to overcome and find victory through vulnerability. I love this book. You will too."

Perry Noble, senior pastor, NewSpring Church, South Carolina

"Clayton's ability to see God as 'stronger' no matter what personal circumstances weigh against him is one of the characteristics I've admired about him through all the years I've known him. I saw it the first moment I heard him speak and I see it in him today through his support as a personal friend. What you will discover in this book will help you walk through whatever challenges are thrown your way. Read this book and then get a second copy for a friend."

Steven Furtick, lead pastor, Elevation Church; *New York Times* bestselling author of *Crash the Chatterbox*, *Greater*, and *Sun Stand Still*

"We at North Greenville University and Dr. Clayton King have the same goal—to always try to get one more saved!

Clayton has done a tremendous job of sharing Jesus Christ through the book and showing how 'you'll be stronger than you were when you leverage your weakness.' This message is indeed a breath of fresh air and makes it clear that we all need to depend on God's strength and not our own."

Dr. Jimmy Epting, president, North Greenville University

"Clayton has written an inspiring work that helps us glorify God amid adversity. Whether entering, in the middle of, or exiting a difficult time, this book will guide you to find eternal grace beyond your earthly circumstances. In this life, we all encounter difficult times that make this book a must-read for everyone."

Thomas White, president and professor of theology, Cedarville University

"*Stronger* is genuinely authentic, brutally honest, and refreshingly transparent. It is also painful and yet healing, sorrowful and yet hopeful. Many will be encouraged and helped by this book in which my friend Clayton King lays bare his soul and, in the process, shows us the wonderful grace and mercy of God that is available to all who run to him as Father."

Daniel L. Akin, president, Southeastern Baptist Theological Seminary

"I've known Clayton since 1999. I love him. He's been a friend and brother to me. My life is stronger because of him. In the pages of *Stronger*, you not only will meet my friend and brother, you will also meet the God who has forged Clayton into the man he is today. And your life will be stronger too."

Derwin L. Gray, lead pastor, Transformation Church; author of *The High Definition Leader*

"So often, self-centered theology shouts the lie that God desires to shelter his children from any form of adversity. Clayton King, however, shouts back loud and clear that God often ordains and actually uses adversity in the lives of his beloved to grow them in their faith. What a needed message."

David Nasser, author of *Jumping through Fires*

"Clayton King's *Stronger* is a fine little book on the way God uses our weakness to glorify himself and strengthen us. Full of Scripture, stories, and memorable wisdom. Highly recommended."

Bruce Riley Ashford, provost and dean of the faculty, associate professor of theology and culture, Southeastern Baptist Theological Seminary

"In this very personal book, Clayton King opens his heart to reveal a real-life story of ongoing transformation from utter human weakness to incomparable strength—by God's power and grace. You will laugh and you will cry as King shares stories from his life that will help you embrace your human weakness and brokenness as gifts, and welcome the hard knocks of life that bring us to our knees so that God can pick us up and shape in us strength of character and faith. Of those writers who use simple words to paint poignant pictures of enduring truth, *Stronger* is evidence once again that King is among the best."

Evans P. Whitaker, PhD, president, Anderson University

STRONGER

HOW HARD TIMES REVEAL
GOD'S GREATEST POWER

////////// CLAYTON KING

BakerBooks

a division of Baker Publishing Group
Grand Rapids, Michigan

Published by Baker Books
a division of Baker Publishing Group
P.O. Box 6287, Grand Rapids, MI 49516-6287
www.bakerbooks.com

Printed in the United States of America

Library of Congress Cataloging-in-Publication Data
King, Clayton, 1972–
    Stronger : how hard times reveal God's greatest power / Clayton King.
        pages cm
    Includes bibliographical references.
    ISBN 978-0-8010-1684-4 (pbk.)
    1. Suffering—Religious aspects—Christianity. I. Title.
BV4909.K56 2015
248.8′6—dc23   2015002036

The author is represented by The FEDD Agency, Inc.

15 16 17 18 19 20 21   7 6 5 4 3 2

CONTENTS

FOREWORD

I've always appreciated honesty. In almost any and every context, I feel better when I'm dealing with people who don't beat around the bush or sugarcoat the truth. As a pastor, I also want to make sure I am being honest with the people I shepherd and serve. I don't want to give them any false sense of hope that, if they are following Jesus, their lives will be easy and all their bills will be paid and they'll never get sick and their kids will turn out perfectly. I know these things aren't true for me, and they're not true for others either.

So I try to strike a balance between being truthful and being hopeful. I don't just want to warn people of the tough times they will inevitably face in life. I want them to pitch their tent in the land of hope, especially during seasons of weakness and struggle. Because I value this approach to both life and ministry, I respect others who face life's struggles and hardships with the same perspective, especially leaders who influence and instruct those under their care. That's why I resonate so much with Clayton's message in *Stronger*. It is truthful and it is hopeful.

I'd heard about Clayton for several years before we met. He had a reputation as a great communicator and a straight shooter. Then I had a chance to meet him and hear his heart for his marriage to Sharie, his calling to communicate the good news of the gospel, and his desire to help people find hope in hard times. There's a total lack of pretense with Clayton, and that comes through clearly as he tackles one of humanity's greatest mysteries here: whether or not anything good can come out of weakness, suffering, and hardship.

Clayton doesn't flinch. He doesn't even blink. He bares his soul with a combination of pastoral care and reckless abandon. He plays the part of a trusted old friend you can always turn to, then he lets you see his wounds—like the dark season in his life when he watched almost all of his family members die, one after another, culminating in the loss of his father.

Yet *Stronger* is not some kind of sad, sentimental memoir. It's a joyful journey away from despair and toward joy. This is a book that everyone can relate to, because everyone struggles. Somehow, Clayton shows us how to see beyond, almost through, our hard times and into the promise of better days and a stronger future. In no way is this a trite little self-help guide filled with one-liners about "taking the lemons of life and turning them into lemonade." These lessons were born in the crucible of real life, real pain.

Clayton has the guts to share with you, the reader, the very hard questions he asked when it seemed like the sun would never shine again in his life. He faced depression and despair, looked them square in the face, and survived the ordeal with a greater understanding of God's goodness and our ability to grow stronger not just in spite of but because of our weakness.

This book is more than a page-turner. It's a game-changer. It's courageous. It's bold. It's vulnerable and funny and redemptive. It's a revolutionary way to see suffering, which Jesus modeled two thousand years ago.

You will learn that no one is exempt from difficulty. We don't get a pass when it comes to pain. But we can worship God in our weakness because pain has a way of clearing out the clutter in our lives. It burns off the excess and allows us to see what really matters after all: the people we love, the message we carry, and the God we worship.

Mark Batterson, pastor and author
of *The Circle Maker* and *The Grave Robber*

INTRODUCTION

It was mid-April and I was neck-deep in the writing process for the book you hold in your hands right now. My deadline was approaching and I was writing bits and excerpts any chance I could get. So while I waited to board a small plane to Ohio, where I would be preaching for the next three days, I stole away for a few moments in an attempt to bank another few hundred words.

I found the entire ordeal of writing this book to be both spiritually cathartic and emotionally exhausting. In order to write well, I was going to have to dig deep into my raw, wounded soul and dredge up feelings I would rather leave buried. I was attempting to chronicle my own odyssey of weakness for others' benefit, to show everyone how God can leverage bad things for good purposes. It proved to be harder than I imagined.

Over the course of twelve years, I lost nine close family members. When I say "lost," I mean they died. That's an average of one death every sixteen months. I preached each of their funerals too. These included my two grandparents, my wife's grandparents, an uncle, two aunts, and my own mother and father, who died eighteen months apart from each other.

Revisiting those moments of depression and despair felt at times exhilarating (like one feels after a good thirty-minute cry) and at other times like a lobotomy of the heart. Often I would remind myself of A. W. Tozer's famous quote about how God cannot use someone greatly until he has wounded them deeply. If that were true, then I believed God would use this book in a profound way because I had been wounded in a profound way.

///////

As a writer, I've always believed that *intent precedes content*. My intent was to open myself up to the world, for all our sakes, and show readers like you how pain can have a purpose, how weakness can lead to worship, and how brokenness can lead to blessing. I thought the content of these pages would flow from my intention to help others find hope in hard times. But it was tough to get started. Just when I thought I was moving forward, I had to wake up all the old monsters: anxiety, discouragement, grief, regret, and fear. I wanted to tap into the reality of my own weakness to help you face yours. And that kind of thing can't be faked. I would have to kick the hornets' nest.

I had my laptop out and was pounding the keys, working on the chapter dealing with vulnerability, when our plane began to board. I shut down and packed up. And then I received a phone call from my uncle. He was informing me that his wife, my aunt Gwen, had died a few hours earlier. I was sucker punched in the heart. *Not again! Dear God, not again.* Gwen was like a mother to me. She and my father were the best of friends and the closest of siblings. Now she was dead too, less than two years after I buried my dad. And, of course, I would preach her funeral in three days.

So I boarded the plane and began writing again—not on my laptop but in my journal. My ears were ringing and my heart was pounding and my stomach was churning, but I managed to scribble a few things on those pages while the wound was still fresh and pouring blood. For the next three days in Ohio, these words sustained me, and I believe they came straight from the Spirit of God to my weak and wounded soul. Here is what I wrote, verbatim, in my journal that day.

Hard times don't make me happy, but by God's grace, they can make me holy.

Where there's no death, there can be no resurrection. Where there's no cross, there can be no empty tomb.

Peace isn't the absence of crisis. It's the presence of Christ in my crisis.

Just because I feel invisible, it doesn't mean I'm not valuable.

God works in our weakness because that's all he has to work with.

Before every triumph, there is a trial. Before every testimony, there is a test.

I can't stop when I feel stuck. I have to keep moving forward in faith that Jesus is stronger.

I want to give up, but if I'm not dead, then God's not done. If I'm still *breathing*, then I can keep *going*.

I don't have to feed every feeling. Just because I'm lonely, it doesn't mean that God has left me.

I can grow bitter or I can become better. If my pain serves the purpose of seeing Jesus more clearly and preaching the gospel more boldly, then I want to embrace it, not escape it.

I keep asking Jesus to give me something, but he keeps trying to show me something. Maybe the real gift is the revelation of his presence in my pain.

I should stop seeking happiness in my weakness and start seeking holiness. Pain has a way of purifying my motives and clarifying my calling.

God is not punishing me for failure. He is pruning me for fruitfulness.

The things that *break me* are the things that *bring me* closer to God.

Then I remembered 1 Peter 1:6–7, which reads:

In all this you greatly rejoice, though now for a little while you may have had to suffer grief in all kinds of trials. These have come so that the proven genuineness of your faith—of greater worth than gold, which perishes even though refined by fire—may result in praise, glory and honor when Jesus Christ is revealed.

Could those verses apply to my situation? Could I really praise God in my pain? Could it really purify my faith and bring honor and glory to God somehow?

I reached into my backpack and pulled out *Walking with God through Pain and Suffering* by Tim Keller, which I was reading to help me along my own journey as well as a resource for *Stronger*. I randomly flipped to page 8. God must have orchestrated the whole thing, because I read these words:

> The biblical understanding of a fiery furnace is more what we would call a "forge." Anything with that degree of heat is, of course, a very dangerous and powerful thing. However, if used properly, it does not destroy. Things put into the furnace properly can be shaped, refined, purified, and even beautified. This is a remarkable view of suffering, that if faced and endured with faith, it can in the end only make us better, stronger, and more filled with greatness and joy. Suffering, then, actually can use evil against itself. It can thwart the destructive purposes of evil and bring light and life out of darkness and death.[1]

As the plane took off from the runway, I was filled with a tangible, concrete sense of hope. I was going to make it. And by God's grace, I would do more than just *make it*. I would allow God to *make me*—make me a stronger man who knew how to rely on his strength and not my own. I began to see that as God was breaking me, he was actually making me into a man more like his own Son, Jesus Christ.

Just as smooth seas don't create skilled sailors, an easy life has no power to purify us and make us stronger. Hard times, on the other hand, have the power to transform us in ways that no other force could. God leverages them to grab our attention, humble us, teach us to trust him for provision, and use our stories of weakness to help others in their own fiery furnace.

So I'm laying it all out on the table for you: the pain I've felt, the crippling depression, the fits of anxiety, the lessons and the holy moments . . . all of it, raw and unfiltered. May you be filled with hope and promise and encouragement as you see the bigger picture and the better purpose in your hard times. From the outset, you can trust this truth: the comeback may be harder than the setback, but you'll be stronger than you were when you leverage your weakness to find God's strength.

Sometimes God will *remove* the weakness and sometimes he will *redeem* the weakness, but he will never waste your weakness.

BROKENNESS

A Strange Kind of Blessing

God uses men who are weak and feeble enough
to lean on him.

Hudson Taylor, missionary to China

To be human is to be broken. Bones break. Hearts
break. Wills break. Spirits break. Waves break too . . .
sometimes over us and sometimes against us. Sometimes they break over and over again; we are tiny creatures
up against a vast and raging sea, often in over our heads. The
day breaks too, but the nights can be so very long.

We forget that we are fragile, vulnerable creatures, subject
to the elements of time and chance, heat and cold, hunger
and desire. We forget because before we suffer, we live under

the delusion that we are stronger than we really are. We are the stars of the movie that plays in our heads, dreaming we are smarter, tougher, and more durable than we are. We may bend. We stub our toe, we scrape our knee . . . and then we mend.

But then there are these moments, every so often, when life does not bend us. It breaks us. Sometimes we break ourselves. And there is no running from the scene of the accident. All of a sudden we realize how broken, how fragile, how dependent

> *Weakness is a welcome sign hanging on the door of our lives, inviting God inside.*

we really were all along, and that we were not as strong as we thought we were. And when we do finally taste the bitter salt of the waves that have broken over us, we are awakened to the fact that the world itself, even in its staggering beauty, is so very broken—that we are in fact surrounded by people who are as broken as we are. The world didn't break because we finally tasted our own weakness—rather we see our pain illuminated in the world and recognize that it already is and always has been broken.

I have no idea in what ways you are or have been broken, nor why. I don't know where the cracks and tears are in your heart or on your body, what wounds have been inflicted on you or that you have inflicted on yourself. I only know that, in ways that are more profound than you can possibly imagine right now, God makes himself known in and through our brokenness. Weakness is a welcome sign hanging on the door of our lives, inviting God inside.

It is not our goal to see how broken we can become, as if brokenness in and of itself is a virtue. No. But what I do believe is this: that the God offered to us in Jesus of Nazareth has been broken for us and has been torn in all the ways we are tearing. And that somehow, mysteriously, in our own brokenness there is a way to connect with God from where we are. As hard as it is for us to comprehend right now, embracing the brokenness of the moment we're in is actually the path to strength and wholeness.

But let's not skip ahead too quickly. Before the day breaks, there is much to learn from the darkness we are in right now. Rather than patting you on the head and telling you everything will be all right in the morning, I want to take you with me into my own experience of night and shine a flashlight on my own brokenness—so you will know you aren't alone in yours.

A Rude Awakening

It was the darkest day of my life. One of my worst nightmares had just come true. And it was only the beginning. I was embarking on a journey of suffering in which my world would be turned on its head. I was on my way to discovering my own weakness, trading strength for fragility. As it turns out, this was also a voyage of learning about God, life, and the world in ways I could not have dreamed of before. I had no idea it would be so *traumatic*. And I had no idea it would be so *transforming*. The only thing harder than telling my story is keeping it bottled up inside.

I travel for a living. Technically, I make a living as a minister— but my job requires that I travel, so I actually *preach* for a living.

As an itinerant speaker and author, I live my life on the move from one church (or university, camp, or retreat center) to the next. I'm that guy who lives out of a suitcase and sleeps in Hampton Inns and Hiltons. And I've been living this lifestyle since I was just fourteen years old.

The way it all started might sound unbelievable. But my story is my story, and I suppose most of our stories have something strange and spectacular somewhere along the way. So believe it or not, on the night I first converted to faith in Jesus Christ, God clearly called me to preach. Not once, but twice. And it was not a metaphorical or allegorical call. It was clear and real and tangible.

I was at a small, rural church in South Carolina. Those kinds of churches have an altar down at the front of the church for people to come and pray in response to the preacher's invitation. That night the guest evangelist preached a message asking us to repent of our sins and commit our lives to Jesus. Even though I came from a religious family in a religious town and attended church routinely, that was the night I knew I wanted to really become a Christian for myself. So along with a number of other teenagers, I went down to the altar to ask Jesus to take control of my life.

That's when it happened the first time. As I was kneeling at the altar and praying to God to save me, I thought I heard a voice talk back to me—out loud. I was expecting my prayer to be more of a monologue, not a dialogue in which God responded. The tone wasn't pushy or forceful. It was calm and its volume was normal. The man's voice said, "Preach the gospel." I couldn't tell if it was in my head or a real person speaking. I was just a kid!

I turned my head to see who would be so audacious as to speak out loud during such a holy moment. Who would dare interrupt me while I was literally asking Jesus into my heart? He obviously didn't understand church etiquette. But when I looked behind me, there was no man. My eyes only registered a couple dozen other teenagers—all about my age and all with their heads down and their eyes closed, evidently asking Jesus to save them too. None of them seemed to have heard the voice I heard. Was I hearing things? Had I imagined it?

As I rode home in the church van with teenagers I had known from childhood, I was vividly aware that something had changed in me. I felt very different than I had felt just a few hours earlier. The van dropped me off at my front door and I entered the familiarity of home. The smell of supper still hung in the air. It was winter and the wood-burning stove hummed in the den, accompanied by the faint smell of smoke. I said hello to my parents and slipped upstairs to my bedroom as if controlled by an unseen force, and slid down on my knees beside my bed. I sensed that I had unfinished business to attend to, business that had begun an hour earlier at the church altar.

Praying on my knees was not a personal habit. I had *never* prayed on my knees before that night. Now I was there for the second time, with carpet fibers pressing through my jeans into my bony kneecaps. An awkward place to find myself, to be sure, especially with no real experience of what to do or even how to pray—how to speak to a God who had just become as real to me as the blanket on my bed where I rested my elbows.

I picked up where I'd left off back at the church. This time it was just me, all alone in my bedroom, so I felt more comfortable praying out loud, which helped me focus my thoughts and emotions. It's odd to me that nearly three decades later I can still remember what I prayed that night.

"Jesus, I know you're real. I know that you just came into my life. I don't know what all that means or even what you want me to do next, but here and now, Lord Jesus, I give you everything. I want to tell people about you. I will go anywhere. I will do anything. I will pay any price to follow you." It was a tender and vulnerable moment for me, perhaps the most meaningful moment of my life up until that point. Then it happened again . . . that voice.

"Preach the gospel."

It was that same voice from the church saying the same thing it had said earlier. I never saw a face. But I heard that voice. Then it made sense. *His voice was not interrupting me. He was answering me.* I was praying to Jesus and Jesus was responding to my prayer. Like a normal conversation with a friend, requiring two people to talk to each other, I was talking to God. I just wasn't expecting him to talk back. But he did. And what seemed like an interruption was actually an invitation. Jesus was inviting me to join him on a journey. He was inviting me to walk with him in a relationship in which I would feel fantastic joy, elation, severe suffering, and real weakness.

You may bristle at the thought of God speaking to anyone today. I understand that. And I don't blame you. It's odd. Maybe crazy. It doesn't happen to most people like that. But I sensed Jesus calling me to preach the gospel. And I guess he had the right to, since I told him I would do anything he wanted me to do. That night was the moment that changed my life. Prior to it I was a typical kid with a big mouth who loved to entertain crowds of people, play sports, and get into trouble. After that moment I was filled with a sense of purpose. I began to see why I was put on the earth. I was going to tell people about Jesus. I was going to preach about how good God was and how God could change lives.

Immediately, doors began opening for me to speak. As an eighth grader I was invited to speak in local churches and youth groups. Then I started teaching on Sunday nights at a local prison, before I was even old enough to drive. Then I began preaching at youth rallies where I was the same age as or younger than most of the people I was speaking to. I started making the rounds in our region of South Carolina. I was a high-school football player at one of the largest high schools in our state, which gave me a huge platform. Then I gained some more credibility when I became an officer in the National Beta Club, an organization for smart kids.

Things were going great! By the time I was a senior, I was living the dream. I was team captain, student body president, had been recruited by a dozen colleges for both football and academics, and was speaking at bigger and bigger events and seeing more and more people respond to the gospel. Things

To me, strength and success were proof that God was using me and that he loved me.

were good. Really good. I felt like my faith was growing deeper. I felt *strong*. It was during this season that I subconsciously began making a big assumption: God's power in my life was most evident when I was strong—strong in my faith, strong in ministry, strong in athletics and academics.

To me, strength and success were proof that God was using me and that he loved me.

I was physically strong. I was six feet three and 215 pounds. I was competitive and in shape. I was a decent football player who could knock heads off. I was academically strong. I graduated at the top of my class and was set to go to college on a full academic scholarship. I was spiritually strong. During my senior year in high school I was preaching multiple times a week. My parents supported me. My pastor mentored and affirmed me. I was reading the Bible daily.

Essentially, I was enjoying a season of God's blessing. I hadn't experienced hard times in my life yet. Moreover, I assumed that becoming a Christian was a guarantee of sorts. Jesus would save my soul but he would also bless my life by making things easy for me. There was a subtle shift taking place in my perspective. I assumed that being in ministry at such a young age meant that God would insulate me from hard times and protect me from the trials and tests that everyone else had to go through. Didn't he owe that to me? If I was going to give up all my other hopes and aspirations to work for him, the least he could do was provide a struggle-free life so that I could accomplish more for his kingdom. Or so I thought.

When the Nightmare Comes to Pass

Fast-forward about two decades. It was November 2010. The energetic high-school evangelist had matured into a husband and a dad who was still passionate about preaching the gospel. Yet in the process I had learned some hard lessons and won some hard-fought battles. I was discovering that being a Christian contained no promises of an easy life. The call to preach the gospel carried its own set of burdens along with its blessings. And just when I thought I had graduated to the next level of my understanding of God and life and ministry, the bottom fell out of my life and I began freefalling into a bottomless pit of despair and depression.

My parents were both getting older and sicker. My mother had a chronic kidney issue. My father was diabetic and suffered from heart disease. I lived an hour away from them, but they kept me well informed of their infirmities. So every time I traveled anywhere overnight, I wrestled with a very real fear that one of them would die while I was traveling and I wouldn't be there to help. But ten thousand times greater than that fear was the nightmare that one of my parents would die while I was out of the country, and I would be stuck on foreign soil with no way to get back to my family. And that's exactly what happened. My worst nightmare came true. And it was just the beginning.

I've been to almost forty nations, including India, Egypt, Malaysia, and Russia. It's common for me to be out of the country, usually preaching or leading a mission trip. But this particular trip, to Canada, was for a TV appearance to promote a new book. I flew from Charlotte to Toronto on a Sunday afternoon. Before our departure, I called home from the airport to check on my dad. My mom answered and we talked for a few minutes. When I hung up, it never occurred to me that we would never speak again on this earth.

When I landed in Toronto a couple of hours later and turned my phone back on, text messages began flooding in from my brother, informing me that something had happened to Mom. There was a voicemail from my dad. It was barely intelligible. He was screaming and crying and asking me to pray for Mom. My world started spinning. My heart rate immediately doubled and I broke out in a sweat. While the plane was still moving down the runway toward the gate, I called my dad. He was a basket case. All I could decipher was that he had found my mom lying on the floor. The ambulance came and took her to the hospital, but he thought she was already dead when she left the house. My brother was with her in the emergency room.

Can you imagine what it was like for me to have that conversation with my dad while sitting on the runway in an airplane, in a middle seat, with two total strangers sitting on either side of me . . . in another country? I remember hoping that it was just a bad dream I would wake up from, but I never woke up. It wasn't a dream, and it was going to get even worse.

///////

My brother wasn't answering his phone. I continued calling him without success. Then we had to go through Canadian customs, where I was not allowed to even have my phone in my hand. There was a terrorist threat. None of us were allowed to hold our phones until we cleared customs, which would take over an hour. I felt it buzz in my pocket and knew my brother was calling me from the hospital, but when I went to answer it a customs officer yelled at me and threatened to take my phone away from me. I couldn't even look at my phone to find out if my mom was alive or dead. For sixty minutes I felt like I was losing my mind. I prayed a lot during that hour.

God, a little help here?
Lord, I've been faithfully following you for twenty-four years. Do you think you could heal my mom?

God, why are these custom officers so mean? I told them my mom was dying back home and they ignored me and walked away.

Jesus, why is this happening to my mom? Why is this happening to my dad? Why is this happening to me?

God, please don't let my mom die while I'm in another country. If you love me, you will heal her and get her home.

If my mom is dead, who will take care of my dad?

My entire understanding of strength and weakness was being turned upside down. It was the first time in my life that I felt completely out of control. There wasn't a single thing I could do. The only person I could talk to was God. And I was terrified. I vividly remember calling out to God while standing in that line in Toronto. *Jesus, I've never felt more afraid or more helpless. Please heal my mom. Don't let her die. Please comfort my dad. Please be near my brother as he waits for news from the doctors.*

Suddenly I was overcome with a crystal clear thought. *We are all completely weak. We are all so very broken. Each of us is powerless to do or change anything.* My mom was possibly dead in a hospital room back in South Carolina. My brother was alone in the waiting room, anticipating news from the doctors. My terminally ill father was home alone, unable to even walk, awaiting news about his wife. I was standing helplessly in a customs line at a Canadian airport. It was the first time I remember feeling complete terror and absolute weakness. Finally, I was feeling my own brokenness.

The Vortex of Weakness and Despair

What do you do when you find yourself in a situation far outside of your ability? What do you say when you know for certain that you are too weak to change any detail of circumstances that are way beyond your control? And how do you move forward when you're facing an obstacle that's impossible to defeat? Furthermore, as a Christian, how do you approach your own weakness in the face of a foe you can't possibly hope to overcome? How do you square up God's unlimited power with your own inability to gain victory over discouragement, depression, debt, disease, and death?

I've had to come face-to-face with these hard questions, and it hasn't been easy. There are no quick answers. It's a lot tougher than reciting positive phrases or quoting your favorite Bible verses. And if you haven't already had to deal with these questions head-on, you will at some point. If you live long enough, you're going to face hard times too. They may not be exactly like the ones I've endured, but they're coming

Sometimes hard times don't mean that you're messing up. They mean that you're growing up.

your way eventually. And when those storms hit you, they will shake you to your core. They will wreck you emotionally and cause you to question all you've ever believed in. You may get so frustrated that you scream at God. I know I did.

Yet within that vortex of weakness and despair lies a very tangible and real hope. When all that you held on to as stable and predictable starts to crumble around you, you will find a new strength that springs out of your weakness. It will overcome you and lift you up when you least expect it and most need it. It's a strange paradox; when you are weak, you can actually tap into a secret reserve of strength that God has stored up for you. Sometimes hard times don't mean that you're messing up. They mean that you're growing up.

Sucker Punched

I finally made it through customs. I called my dad but all he could do was weep and wail. I thought he was having a nervous breakdown. He was home alone while my brother was at the ER. My heart broke when my dad said to me, "Son, I just wish you were here right now with me. I'm so scared, I don't know what to do." I called my brother. No answer. I was walking outside, along the sidewalk, to meet my driver who would take me to the hotel in Toronto. That's when I got the text from my brother.

She didn't make it.

I stopped dead in my tracks. The icy November wind cut through me like a knife. My mother was dead in South Carolina and I was in Canada. My worst nightmare had come true. I lost all control of my emotions and began to sob from a place deep down inside my stomach. I had to tell my driver, a total stranger, that my mom was dead. Then I walked back inside the airport. I had to get back home. My dad and my brother needed me, and I needed them. I needed my wife and my sons by my side. It was 9:00 p.m. and I knew it would be nearly impossible to get back to Charlotte that night. The ticket agent was compassionate, but there were no flights out of Toronto until 6:00 a.m. the next morning. I would have to spend the night in Canada. In a hotel room. By myself.

That's when I fell down on the floor, right at the ticket counter. All the strength left my body. I couldn't even compose myself enough to stand up. I just lost it. I wept uncontrollably. I wanted to throw up. People were staring at me. I was an emotional mess. A police officer came over to investigate, but the ticket agent motioned for him to stand back and leave me alone. All I had in that moment was a suitcase and a computer bag. And a broken heart. For a brief moment I wanted to stop living.

Yet a strange thing happened in the midst of such despair. I knew that I had to get up. I couldn't stay on that floor forever. I composed myself, prayed a simple, desperate prayer to God asking for help, and managed to get up on one knee. Then I leaned on my suitcase and got my other knee underneath me. I thanked the ticket agent, grabbed my boarding pass for the flight the next morning, and walked back outside into the frigid wind to find my driver, who took me to the hotel. I called my wife and broke the news to her. Then I told my children that their grandma was dead. We all cried together. I just wanted to hold each of them in my arms but a thousand miles separated us.

When I walked into that lonely hotel room, I did something I had grown accustomed to since that night at the little church where I was saved: I fell on my knees beside the bed. I called out to Jesus for help and cried until my eyes swelled shut. I told him how weak and helpless I felt. I asked him for strength. And he responded. I felt a strange sensation, like the way I felt twenty-four years earlier in my bedroom as a teenager when I sensed God calling me to preach. I felt his tangible presence as I knelt in that hotel room, comforting me, holding me.

Friends began to call me. They prayed for me, read verses to me, and encouraged me. One of my closest friends called and peeled back the years to his adolescence, when he lost his mom when he was twelve. He got real and raw with me; he talked about his hurt, confusion, and anger with God. He walked me through all of his emotions and gave me permission to embrace the grief I was feeling. Then I called my dad and attempted to minister to him, even though I had no idea what to say. But God began to give me words for him. In my weakness, I felt God's strength working through the phone. Oddly enough, I felt weak and strong at the same time.

That night didn't last forever. Morning came, and I boarded the plane and flew back home. I drove to my dad's house and cried all day with him and my brother. We looked at pictures of my mother, Jane King. We told stories about her, laughed and remembered, and cried some more. I preached her funeral two days later, managing to say a few words here and there in between outbursts of sobbing and weeping. I knew my dad wouldn't survive much longer. We had thought he would die first because of his diabetes.

Just a few days after she died, it was Thanksgiving. Two days later, it was my birthday. Three days after that, it was my mom's birthday. Then just two days later, it was my brother's birthday. Can you imagine how hard it was to absorb all of that in just over a week? Without the woman who held our family together? I ran out of tears.

And then . . . life continued. I knew I couldn't stay in that pit of grief forever. I had to find a way to live again.

The Light through the Cracks

As I struggled to find my way, some words from 2 Corinthians carried me through my dark night. I find it one of the most fascinating books in the New Testament because the apostle Paul wrote it from his own place of brokenness. The people at the church in Corinth, whom he loved and had given his life for, were spurning him in favor of the so-called super-apostles, the first-century equivalent of money-grubbing preachers, who dazzled gullible people with their fancy show.

Throughout the letter, you can feel Paul's heartbreak that these people whom he'd laid down his life for were now picking religious con artists over him. He was unafraid to let his humanity show. He was not only concerned for their souls, he was struggling with his own sense of rejection. Here he was, beaten and battered by all the talk about how these other religious leaders were more impressive than him, better looking than him, and better speakers than him. His beloved friends at Corinth should have taken his side, but they didn't. Paul had suffered through numerous physical beatings, but this situation beat his soul. So throughout this letter, we get the heart of a weathered, lovesick apostle, still hanging on because of the people he can't get out of his heart or his head.

Paul has shaped so much of not only Christianity but also Western culture with his words. Even at the time, Paul had a pedigree like nobody else's and a list of accomplishments a mile long he could use to mount his counterattack, to convince these people he cared so deeply for that he was the one they should listen to. But instead Paul did the strangest thing: he kept talking about his weakness. He put his brokenness on display for all of them to see.

In one of the most crucial texts of the letter, Paul said:

> For we do not proclaim ourselves; we proclaim Jesus Christ as Lord and ourselves as your slaves for Jesus' sake. For it is the God who said, "Let light shine out of darkness," who has shone in our hearts to give the light of the knowledge of the glory of God in the face of Jesus Christ.
>
> But we have this treasure in clay jars, so that it may be made clear that this extraordinary power belongs to God and does not come from us. We are afflicted in every way, but not crushed; perplexed, but not driven to despair; persecuted, but not forsaken; struck down, but not destroyed; always carrying in the body the death of Jesus, so that the life of Jesus may also be made visible in our bodies. (2 Cor. 4:5–10 NRSV)

In a stroke of pure genius, Paul compared how the power of God shone through his weakness to the light that shone from a flame through thin clay pottery.

Corinth was known for manufacturing cheap clay lamps. Precisely because of their thinness, these vessels cast more light. This frail form also made it clear that the light came from another source, so Paul added that in his case, frailty

---

We can never escape our weakness.
So we must embrace it.

---

ought to make it more obvious that the power came from God and not himself. "But we have this treasure in clay jars, so that it may be made clear that this extraordinary power belongs to God and does not come from us" (v. 7 NRSV). The more cracked we are, the more the light of Jesus is revealed in our brokenness.

None of us like to feel broken. We want to feel strong, in charge, full of courage. We want to stop feeling so frail, so human—we wish we could be unaffected by the pain of the world in and around us. We would not choose to be crushed, to feel rejected, to feel spurned. We would not choose to be heartbroken. But we don't get to choose what breaks us. We only get to choose how we respond. We can never *escape* our weakness. So we must *embrace* it.

It is precisely because we are so broken that there will be no confusion about where the light comes from. It will clearly be the gift of God, and not of ourselves. As lamps, we may feel like cheap, thin, transparent earthen vessels similar to the ones manufactured so long ago in Corinth. But God sends us out into a dark world, where everyone around us has their own pain and brokenness to contend with and so many are walking and living in darkness, desperate for light. That world needs to see God through our weakness more than through our strength. It's remarkable, almost comical, how effectively God uses our own hard times and brokenness to help others. As my pastor once said, Jesus uses losers. It's all he really has to work with.

More than any other passage in 2 Corinthians though, I began to meditate on one particular passage I had read many times before. It had always caught me off-guard as being a bit mysterious, even mystical. But I couldn't quit thinking about it—like a scratched vinyl record that kept skipping back to the same part. It was this short passage that would change my perspective on hard times, weakness, and strength:

In order to keep me from becoming conceited, I was given a thorn in my flesh, a messenger of Satan, to torment me. Three times I pleaded with the Lord to take it away from me, but he said to me, "My grace is sufficient for you, for *my power is made perfect in weakness.*" Therefore I will boast all the more gladly about my weaknesses, so that Christ's power may rest on me. That is why, for Christ's sake, I delight in weaknesses, in insults, in hardships, in persecutions, in difficulties. *For when I am weak, then I am strong.* (12:7–10, emphasis added)

Hard times reveal God's greatest power. His strength is made perfect in our weakness. And his Word can show us how Paul arrived at the place of embracing his brokenness as a blessing, because it wasn't always the case for him. But for right now, I want you to know that whatever broken place you are in, God will meet you there. Pretending that you are not weak is no shortcut to wholeness. Right now, what you need to know is that grace is present in the midst of your hard time. His grace is sufficient for you. His power is made perfect in weakness.

Wishful thinking will not get you out of your brokenness. Clicking your heels together three times and saying "I'm not really broken" won't make it any better. We spend so much time trying to escape our weakness when our first task really should be to allow God to be fully present with us in it. We have to stop trying so desperately to get out of where we are just because it feels bad and become aware of how near God is to us right where we are. He is already present in our broken places.

"Blessed are those who mourn," Jesus says, "for they will be comforted" (Matt. 5:4). We cannot receive comfort unless we allow for our tears. God has sent us the Holy Spirit, the very presence of Jesus, as the Comforter, precisely because he knew how desperately we would need comfort. We never know the Spirit as Comforter until we hurt so bad that we need to be comforted.

Henri J. M. Nouwen talked about how we, like Jesus in the Garden of Gethsemane, will all have to drink the cup of suffering in our lives. It is tempting to try to avoid the cup or to not drink it all the way down. But in some mysterious way, it is not that God works in us *despite* our brokenness and pain but that he works *right through* it. The very thing we think might kill us has an odd way of bringing us to life. The very trial that threatens to destroy us may yet be the vehicle for a joy and freedom we have not yet known. But we cannot get to that place unless we hold the cup of sorrow we have been given and drink it all the way down. In Nouwen's words:

> As we gradually come to befriend our own reality, to look with compassion at our own sorrows and joys, and as we are able to discover the unique potential of our way of being in the world, we can move beyond protest, put the cup of our life to our lips and drink it, slowly, carefully but fully . . . we can choose to drink the cup of our life with the deep conviction that by drinking it we will find our true freedom. Thus, we will discover that the cup of sorrow and joy we are drinking is the cup of salvation.[1]

Sometimes brokenness precedes the blessing. And other times brokenness is the blessing. Stop trying to escape it and learn to embrace it, because it's God's way of using you to shine his light, and it's the means by which he is drawn to you with tender love and comfort when you need it most.

HUMILITY

When the Thing That Hurts
You May Actually Help You

But you, Lord, do not be far from me. You are
my strength; come quickly to help me.

Psalm 22:19

God is attracted to weakness. He can't resist those
who humbly and honestly admit how desperately
they need him.

Jim Cymbala, *Fresh Wind, Fresh Fire*

I had no earthly idea how much my mom had been keeping from me. Not only had she been concealing her own
heart disease and kidney failure but she had also been

hiding a prescription drug addiction. As a result of a freak accident in which she broke a bone in her foot, she began using strong narcotics prescribed by a doctor to ease the pain. Because of the increasing stress of caring for my dad, she also began taking the pills to fall asleep. Eventually, the drugs became her only way to escape from a world that was spinning out of control. She thought the pills were helping her survive, but they were killing her.

The drugs became a crutch for her to lean on while she was caring for my dad. Once she was no longer there, he still demanded care, so the weight of taking care of my terminally ill father fell on me and my brother. My mother had been handling all of his daily needs: medicine, meals, bathing, and making sure he got to his dialysis treatments every other day. Then she died. Suddenly we became the caregivers. We had kids of our own. I had a job and a large ministry to lead, and I was also traveling several days a week—all in the midst of transitioning into the final months of my father's life, when he would need round-the-clock help. To pile on the anxiety, our ministry was about to embark on a multimillion-dollar building project. Oh yeah, and I had a book deadline looming on the horizon.

Because my brother was fighting his own personal battles, he wasn't emotionally capable of taking care of my father. To be sure, it was a nearly impossible task for anyone. And it eventually landed on my shoulders.

I lived an hour away from my dad and was traveling three or four days a week preaching while running a large nonprofit ministry. Soon I was also attempting to pay my dad's bills, arrange his in-home care, and take care of his dialysis treatments. He had been completely disabled for years and seldom left the house except for medical procedures. I loved him with all of my heart, and because we were so close, I tried to do anything and everything he needed me to do for him. Even if I knew I couldn't possibly handle it. I noticed myself wearing thin. Anxiety levels were growing. I almost never got more than three hours of sleep at a time. My temper was flaring up with my kids. I was ignoring my relationship with my wife. And my father continued to decline. The sicker he became, the more help he needed from me. I was reaching the end of myself.

Honesty and Humility

I was just beginning to learn about true humility. I realized that the first step was being honest enough to embrace my limits and admit my helplessness. This wasn't exactly easy for me. I'm the guy who has always been able to get things done. I'm a problem-solver. I know how to fix situations. I'm good at rallying a team together to achieve a goal. And I'd grown sinfully proud of my abilities. Suddenly I was facing a situation I couldn't fix.

There was no easy answer to my dad's terminal condition. I watched him slowly deteriorate in front of me, and there was nothing I could do to change any of it. What exacerbated the situation was our history; my dad had taught me how to do all the things I was so proud of being able to do. He had entrusted me with great responsibility, even as a little boy. I worked hard to earn and keep that trust, so he knew what I was capable of. In plain English, there was a clear expectation that I would ride in and save the day and make my dad better. But there was no way I could fix my dad—being so powerless was humbling in and of itself. Even more humbling were the moments when he did need help I could provide. What I share here is not meant to shock you or to be crass in any way. I've learned to fight the fear that my vulnerability will turn people away, because I know that it actually invites people in. So here goes . . .

One of the most unforgettable moments of my life happened in the hospital. It was a terribly difficult day that God leveraged for my good in my journey toward humility. After my dad's first heart surgery, I stayed with him for over a week. In the middle of the night, he became restless and wanted to get up and take a shower. It was 3:30 a.m. He asked me to help get him up and into the bathroom. Groggy and dazed, I obliged. As he held himself upright by the handrail in the shower, I scrubbed his body from head to toe, beginning with his hair. But because of the medication he was taking, he couldn't control his bowels. Once they released, he couldn't stop. It was awful. He began weeping, right there in the shower, begging me to forgive him, totally embarrassed at the situation. He apologized profusely and told me to call a nurse to come help clean him up.

But I sensed the Holy Spirit speaking to me too. He was telling me to humble myself and love my dad, to care for him and clean him and console him; to encourage him and stay by his side and not embarrass him further by calling a nurse. As I washed the lower half of my father's body, I thought of all the times he had cleaned me up as a baby, all the times he had cared for me as a boy, and I sensed God breaking down a wall in my heart. It was the wall of pride. It became apparent to me that if I wanted to actually become like Jesus, I would have to suffer and serve like Jesus.

At heart I'm a small-town boy who's never forgotten where he came from, and I've never walked around under the delusion that I'm some kind of a big deal. But the nature of my life and ministry is that I'm often the guy on the stage with a microphone, speaking at the conference or the concert. And while I could regale you with plenty of horror stories from life on the road, slugging it out in little venues in towns you've never heard of, there have also been nice moments when I've been given the seat of honor, treated like a VIP in

It became apparent to me that if I wanted to actually become like Jesus, I would have to suffer and serve like Jesus.

the greenroom, or introduced to other Christian leaders I have admired. The funny thing is, when I'm in my element doing what I do, and there is a real sense that God is using me to connect in a meaningful way to those I'm preaching to, that is where I *look the best* in front of other people (regardless of how I might be falling apart on the inside).

But when you're standing in the shower with your dad, in the filth, cleaning him of his own excrement, life gets reduced to something much more primal than any of those moments allow. Nothing I have ever done—no sermon given, no book written—prepared me for a moment like that. And none of them mattered as much. It is not that I think I did something especially noble for my dad—he had given everything to me, and I don't think he deserved anything less than that. But it was amazing how much that single moment relativized all my other so-called accomplishments. The moments on the stage were important, but they did not define me. Ultimately, the moments we are given to serve in the most awkward, self-abasing ways imaginable are what really make us who we are. I could not have been more "off the radar" of the evangelical Christian world than in that little hospital in Greenville, South Carolina, at 3:30 a.m., wiping my father's waste off his legs and feet.

Isn't it strange how God works? My dad felt like he was losing his manhood, hot tears streaming down his face, while his son was caring for him in a way that was unthinkable to him. But had I ever had a moment in my life when I was able to love him as purely or as well? He was broken, and I was able to care for him the way he cared for me when I

When God is breaking you, he is really making you—making you into a stronger person who understands your own weakness and your reliance on God alone.

was a weak little infant filling up my diaper in a crib. And in the moment when he felt less like a man than ever, God was making me into a man like never before—making me into the strong, loving man I have always known my father to be. When God is breaking you, he is really making you— making you into a stronger person who understands your own weakness and your reliance on God alone.

A Better Question

When times get hard and things feel like they're falling apart, we instinctively ask *why*. You want to know why God is allowing you to hurt, why God doesn't answer your prayers, why God doesn't make things better or easier. But there's a better question. Instead of asking why, you should be asking *what*. What does God want to teach me? What does God want to show me? What does God want to change in me? What is God's ultimate purpose in this pain?

Brokenness is something we all share, whether we want to or not. We can leverage our brokenness as a way of leaning into God but we often have to choose to do so, and choose whether or not we will allow God to actually humble us. The ego is a powerful, self-protective thing, and it fights to keep its life at all costs. Thinkers such as Carl Jung have demonstrated that many of our decisions are motivated by the need to protect our ego. Of course, the Bible has said as much for thousands of years, that our hearts are deceitfully wicked and not to be trusted. The trick of this is that the ego is not the real self to begin with—it's a composite of all the things we wish were true about ourselves, the things we want others and maybe even ourselves to believe.

When Jesus admonishes his audience in Mark 8:34 that "If any want to become my followers, let them deny themselves and take up their cross and follow me" (NRSV), it wasn't some mystical command that would allow them to release their inner god by denying desire. It was a radical call to abandon their own selves as gods to be worshiped and to begin following the one true God who had the audacity and the authority to demand their very lives as his disciples.

That means we have to humble ourselves. And there is a reason that the words *humility* and *humiliation* are so closely related. On one reading, that moment with my father was humiliating for him and for me. But God leverages those moments not to bring shame but to teach us to be dependent, to give us a sense of scale and perspective. We are all fragile, vulnerable creatures whose bodies can be bruised and damaged at any given time. But in those moments, whether we are the one who serves or the one being served, we are reminded of our humanity—and we are humbled. And I've got good news for you: even if the source of your humiliation is self-inflicted, and there is something shameful in your life that brings you low, God can use that too. It's just the way the kingdom of God works. Everything that goes down is going to come back up, and everything that is humbled will one day be exalted. As Jesus said, whoever wants to save their life must lose it by giving it to God (see Mark 8:35).

When we are going through what feels like a living hell, we always want to know if the hard times are ultimately helping us or hurting us. And the answer is nearly always *yes*. Both of those things are happening simultaneously. There is nothing more insidious and destructive than pride, and everything hard we experience means our fragile egos are deconstructed and our pride is exposed and crushed. And that is never a bad thing.

Pride—a sense of self-reliance—forgetting that we are small, dependent creatures in need of God and each other, cuts us off from the source of authentic life. And it's when our pride is exalted that we are heading for a fall. Thus Proverbs 16:18–19 says:

> Pride goes before destruction,
>   a haughty spirit before a fall.
> Better to be lowly in spirit along with the oppressed
>   than to share plunder with the proud.

Falling never sounds like a good idea, right? And yet the irony is, it's when we fall that we are in a position to be exalted. That is the grand reversal of the gospel—the last will be first. What a paradox! As C. S. Lewis once said regarding the end of time and judgment day, "We shall then, for the first time, see every one as he really was. There will be surprises."[1] This is why we can't spend our lives protecting our ego, trying to avoid falls and humiliation at all costs. Sometimes we have to embrace the descent and not resist the things that humble us. The thing that is hurting you is the thing that is humbling you, and the thing that is humbling you is actually helping you to get a clearer view of God's holiness, beauty, and strength.

This is not to say that hard times are always instigated by God. He is not some kind of cosmic schoolmarm out to teach you a lesson through sadistic means. God harnesses the things that humble us. The same things that feel like they are going to kill us are often in the end part of what saves us. Pride is ultimately what is most likely to keep us from a life of love, and therefore a life of joy. Our proud ego hides behind fortresses of bitterness, isolation, and self-reliance. It takes something hard to tear those walls down.

God harnesses the things that humble us. The same things that feel like they are going to kill us are often in the end part of what saves us.

Let's be clear here: I'm not saying you should go running into every hard, humiliating thing you can find. I don't want to spend my entire life in the throes of financial ruin or emotional anxiety any more than you do. And while I find myself inspired by books and movies that depict the heart-wrenching story of someone going from the pit of poverty to the apex of success, I don't personally want to travel that road. Like you, I would much rather just read about those people. I enjoy being inspired by these stories, but I don't want to actually live one of them out. I cheered when William Wallace screamed "Freedom!" at the end of *Braveheart*, and I admired his courage, but I don't want to be disemboweled if I can help it.

If we had our way, we would skip straight to the part of life where we get to live like we're on a perpetual vacation, with plenty of sunshine and a hammock on the beach stretched between two palm trees. We'd rather fast-forward through the hard parts and skip to the easy scenes. That's the good life right there, right? No worries. No hurries. Days without cares and concerns. Healthy, wealthy, and wise, as the old saying goes.

An Interruption Becomes an Invitation

I'd like to interrupt this program to plant a menacing thought in your mind. Don't cringe when I say it. Just imagine that there may be another dimension to life that, when embraced, could be the most powerful and liberating revelation to ever dawn on you. I invite you to consider this new perspective, because there may be more to life than just the good times.

What if hard times aren't designed to be endured but embraced?

What if the hard times we try to avoid are holy moments meant to change us into better people?

What if all the weaknesses we live with every day are not interruptions in a good life but invitations from God to a new reality?

If you'll open your mind and your heart to this possibility, you will see that the hard times in your life are not meaningless. You will see that your weakness is not wasted. You will discover that God can leverage the bad things that happen to you and do something good inside of you. The great British pastor and church leader C. H. Spurgeon, for example, lived with numerous ailments, including a heavy depression that he compared to fighting the mist. Yet in his writings he seems to have stumbled upon the revelation that God's power is revealed in hard times. He said, "Many men owe the grandeur of their lives to their tremendous difficulties."[2] You become stronger when your weakness allows God to be your strength.

Power Made Perfect in Weakness

For a moment, let's return to the apostle Paul, writing 2 Corinthians from his own humble place. This is the passage that I think best captures the idea of how God reveals his power to us in times of trial and testing. Paul had already experienced more hardship and difficulty than most of us will ever endure. And he wrote this letter to a small group of Christians in the ancient Greek city of Corinth. They were struggling too. Paul loved them and wanted to help them in their season of weakness, so toward the end of his lengthy letter to them, he opened up about something he had never told anyone else. He modeled humility when he became vulnerable with his friends about his own hardships, in hopes that they would connect with his example and gain hope that *there is a greater purpose in the pain.*

> In order to keep me from becoming conceited, I was given a thorn in my flesh, a messenger of Satan, to torment me. Three times I pleaded with the Lord to take it away from me, but he said to me, "My grace is sufficient for you, *for my power is made perfect in weakness.*" Therefore I will boast all the more gladly about my weaknesses, so that Christ's power may rest on me. That is why, for Christ's sake, I delight in weaknesses, in insults, in hardships, in persecutions, in difficulties. *For when I am weak, then I am strong.* (2 Cor. 12:7–10, emphasis added)

This passage has received its fair share of attention from scholars and experts. It's been dissected countless times. Entire books have been written trying to explain what Paul was talking about. Sermons are still preached attempting

---

The greater purpose in our weakness is to experience an intimacy in our relationship with God we could never know any other way.

---

to uncover the great mystery of exactly what Paul's "thorn in the flesh" actually was. And the reason why these verses have been so popular for so long is because they speak so directly to the human condition.

Everyone can relate to feeling overwhelmed and weak. We all intuitively want to believe in a greater purpose for the painful and trying seasons we go through. This passage gives us that hope. It provides a firm place for us to plant our feet when the storms of life blow hard against us and threaten to knock us down.

If we can learn anything at all from Paul's personal letter to his friends, we can begin injecting some hope into our hard times. We can begin seeing God's strength at work when we are tapped out and empty of our own strength. When we believe hard times can help us, we can endure almost anything. The greater purpose in our weakness is to experience an intimacy in our relationship with God we could never know any other way.

This perspective, when kept in view, carries us through the darkest days and the longest nights and is leveraged for our good and God's glory. We are stronger because of his strength, and his strength is on display in our weakness.

The Goal

When our second son was born, we entered into a season I barely remember. The reason I can't recall much of what happened is that our little boy, Joseph, did not sleep for the first eight months of his life. He had colic and acid reflux. Our first son had spoiled us rotten, as he had immediately gotten on a feeding and sleeping schedule. He was compliant and agreeable when it came to bedtime. But our second son seldom slept for more than a few hours at a time. I have only two memories of our early months with Joseph.

The first one was the night I dropped him headfirst directly onto the wood floor in his room. He woke up and began screaming, and I went into his room to rock him back to sleep. Apparently I was so tired that I rocked myself to sleep too, because I woke up as my three-month-old was rolling down my legs headfirst toward the floor. We were both wide awake after his head bounced off the floor like a basketball (way to go, Dad).

The second vivid memory I have is connected to one night of watching late-night infomercials while I tried to console my son. He and I were lying on the couch while my wife tried to sleep. I was so sleep deprived that I'd begun weeping openly at anything on TV with emotionally moving music in the background. And since I was up so late with Joseph, I began getting sucked into these dumb commercials that were selling everything from cancer-fighting juicers to elastic bands that strengthened your core while you ate cheeseburgers. It occurred to me . . . nobody was selling anything to make people weaker! Everything they were selling was designed to make us better, prettier, skinnier, or stronger. Nobody actually wanted to be weak! (At that point I cried some more and ate a pint of Breyer's vanilla bean ice cream.)

It's imperative that you understand the goal here. I don't want you to be confused. The goal is *not* to be weak. Weakness is a result of being a fallen, sinful human being in a broken world. The goal is also *not* to pray for more hard times in your life. You've probably learned by now that you don't have to pray for hard times to come. They will come regardless of who you are or where you live. Weakness is simply a way to get to your destination. Hard times are a vehicle to get you to your goal.

The goal is to be stronger. Stronger in your faith. Stronger in your reliance on Jesus. Stronger as a mom, a dad, a witness, a disciple. Stronger in your submission to the lordship of Christ. *The goal is to be stronger. Weakness is God's way of getting you there*. When this revelation becomes your reality, there is nothing you can't endure by God's grace.

Every trial begins to look like training.

Every test becomes a future testimony.

Your biggest mess becomes your signature message.

Hard times can bring holiness.

Weakness becomes your witness to the world that Jesus lives in you and is working in you for a greater purpose.

The wonderful thing about weakness is that it doesn't have to be wasted. God leverages weakness in the lives of Christians to transform us into fully dependent disciples who look to Christ for all our sufficiency, provision, and identity. Suffering can break your selfishness without breaking your spirit. This was Paul's testimony. This is my testimony. And it can be yours too.

What Defines Us?

Fanny Crosby is one of the most well-known authors of Christian hymns. Her songs have been sung by millions of believers throughout the world and have stood the test of time and brought hope and courage to countless congregations. As a young man, I stood beside my parents in church on Sunday mornings and repeated words that were birthed in the mind and heart of Fanny Crosby half a century before I was born. Was there a special anointing on her to write hymns that would resonate in the hearts of so many Christians for so long? Was there an event in her life that made God real to her? What was the source of her inspiration?

Fanny Crosby was not classically trained in an Ivy League school. She didn't have the technical prowess of a concert musician. Her music flowed from a physical failure she had no control over. Her *inspiration* was birthed from an *inability*. Read these words from a poem she wrote when she was only eight years old:

> Oh, what a happy soul I am, although I cannot see!
> I am resolved that in this world contented I will be.
> How many blessings I enjoy, that other people
> don't,
> To weep and sigh because I'm blind, I cannot and I
> won't![3]

Her poetry was born from a painful place. She was blind from infancy and never knew the joy of watching a sunset or gazing on wildflowers in springtime. Yet she had resolved to find contentment in what she could do. What we could call the weakness of blindness she would call the *blessing* of blindness. Weakness in one area led to strength in another. While her eyes were unable to function, her ears became attuned to pitch and tone and melody. She was able to leverage her weakness and turn it into her greatest strength.

Fanny Crosby is just one example of this phenomenon. As a small boy, I remember riding beside my dad in his old pickup truck as he sang along to a song on the radio. One day he looked at me and said, "The man who sings that song is Ronnie Milsap. He also plays the piano. Would you believe that he's blind?" I was amazed as a little boy that a blind man could play the piano. But we all know it's not impossible. How many times have you sung along to a Ray Charles or Stevie Wonder song? They were also blind.

Our weakness doesn't define us. How we respond to our weakness does.

The First Purpose Is Always Humility

I can attest to one obvious byproduct of difficult circumstances, and if you'll revisit the hardest things you've ever gone through, I bet you'll agree. Hard times will humble us. Over and over in my life, God has leveraged hard times for the sake of my humility, and while these moments were unpleasant, they were necessary for my development and growth as a man and as a disciple.

Paul seemed to believe that this was the first and foremost purpose in the painful and ongoing struggle he found himself emerged in. As Paul was about to wrap up his letter to his Corinthian friends and tell them about his thorn in the flesh, he took a slight detour in his train of thought and wandered off into a strange and cryptic story about "a man" who had what appears to be an out-of-body experience. He told the story rather briefly, but with a firm grasp of the basic details.

> I must go on boasting. Although there is nothing to be gained, I will go on to visions and revelations from the Lord. I know a man in Christ who fourteen years ago was caught up to the third heaven. Whether it was in the body or out of the body I do not know—God knows. And I know that this man—whether in the body or apart from the body I do not know, but God knows—was caught up to paradise and heard inexpressible things, things that no one is permitted to tell. (2 Cor. 12:1–4)

Do you see it? Evidently, fourteen years earlier Paul himself experienced an unspeakable revelation of heaven. It could even seem like he had been escorted to heaven by an angelic concierge, perhaps even Jesus himself. This wouldn't be too far of a stretch. After all, Jesus did appear personally to Paul years earlier, when his name was still Saul. I can imagine how arrogant I could have become if Jesus had come to visit me in the same fashion he visited him. Add to that this stunning experience in which Paul was escorted into the "third heaven," where he witnessed things so glorious and otherworldly that he couldn't even mention it for fourteen years. What did he see while he was up there? It must have been awesome. I'm going to ask Paul when I meet him one day, but until then, I'll just have to leave it to my imagination.

The one thing we don't have to wonder about, however, is how this affected him. He became proud and arrogant. He must have considered himself better than those who opposed him. Paul had numerous critics and enemies, and I can imagine how weary he became of their attacks. As he got older, the temptation grew; he began to think of himself in a manner not befitting a servant of Christ. After all, he had seen "inexpressible things" in a "paradise" that no one else had ever seen.

I imagine him thinking, *Who are these people to run their mouths about my ministry? Who do they think they are to criticize me? They have no idea what I've been through and what I've seen. I not only met Jesus face-to-face on the way to Damascus but also got a personal tour of the highest levels of heaven. If they knew who I was, they would respect me. Maybe I need to tell them about my little weekend excursion to paradise! That would shut them up.*

Pride slowly creeps up on us when we begin to think more highly of ourselves than we should. We begin to desire more attention, more affection, more adoration, and more credit. While it's never wrong to need love and encouragement, we easily drift into dangerous territory when we grow jealous of the attention that others are receiving, wishing that attention was directed toward us.

Ironically, we can even become proud of being used by God! Though we know intuitively that God alone decides how he will equip and use us, when we forget that it's his grace alone that accomplishes anything of significance through us, we become self-obsessed. That's when we have to be reminded of who we are in light of who Christ is. God will employ painful things to humble us and get us off our proud perch.

Paul had walked this road. Indeed, he was still on that road when he opened up about his own pride that grew out of being handpicked by God as a special apostle with a gift no one else possessed. Without mincing words, he clearly states that the thorn in his flesh was not random. It had several purposes. The first one? Humility. It reminded him of how weak he truly was without the grace of Jesus Christ.

Press Pause

Maybe the purpose in the pain we're enduring is to press pause on our pride. That's precisely what God was teaching Paul. Is that what he needs to teach us? Could that difficult circumstance you're praying for God to deliver you from actually be exactly what God intends to use in your life to humble you? Could I be asking God to remove something from my life that he is using on purpose to remind me of who he is and who I am not?

We don't always see clearly enough when it comes to our own pride. Neither did Paul. He was actually confused about his "thorn in the flesh." He called it a "messenger of Satan." That sounds demonic. He went on to describe it as some-

---

Could that difficult circumstance you're praying for God to deliver you from actually be exactly what God intends to use in your life to humble you?

---

thing that was sent to torment him. But he also said that this hardship was used by God and became the subject of his boasting, and he delighted in God's refusal to remove it. So the thorn wasn't necessarily a *good thing*. But it produced a *good result*. The things that hurt you may not be good, but God can use them to produce good fruit.

Our struggles are hard but they can keep us humble and make us holy. I'll say it again: they don't have to be good to produce a good result. I don't know about you, but I try to avoid satanic messengers. I pray for God to protect me from those kinds of things. I also make it a general rule to steer clear of things that cause me torment (such as clowns, math, spiders, and cilantro). But this ailment that Paul saw as a demonic aggravation also became the source of something beautiful in his life.

If I had the choice, I would never willfully choose to repeat the dark days I endured when I lost my mom and watched my father deteriorate into a black hole of depression. It was a hard and treacherous season of my life. But what I gained was a crystal clear perspective on the fragility of life, the importance of family, and the reality of my weakness.

When you want to quit, remember: the harder the road, the better the destination. Remind yourself that God has to root out your self-sufficiency and rugged individualism by digging deep into your life and cutting out the cancer of pride. He doesn't purposefully inflict pain on us. He doesn't have to. The fallen world we live in will do that naturally. But what he does do is leverage the hurts we experience in order to help us. That painful thorn may not be a good thing in and of itself, but it can produce the good fruit of humility in a way that nothing else ever could.

We can't always discern what God is doing in the season he's doing it. What sometimes feels like a beating from the devil may turn out to be a blessing from God.

What we pray for God to take away is often the very thing he employs to break us, to humble us, to push us closer to him. The challenge is to learn not to resist being humbled

---

We can't always discern what God is doing in the season he's doing it. What sometimes feels like a beating from the devil may turn out to be a blessing from God.

---

but to embrace it. Just as it was inevitable that Jesus go to the cross, it is inevitable that Christians go through hard times.

That night I helped my dad in the shower, God reminded me of the night before Jesus was crucified:

Jesus knew that the Father had put all things under his power, and that he had come from God and was returning to God; so he got up from the meal, took off his outer clothing, and wrapped a towel around his waist. After that, he poured water into a basin and began to wash his disciples' feet, drying them with the towel that was wrapped around him. (John 13:3–5)

The Son of God assumed the posture of a servant. He shunned titles and took up a towel. He cleaned the dirty feet of the men he dearly loved. He was humble enough to take a low position in the upper room just hours before he would embrace ultimate weakness on the cross. Yet he was never stronger than when he was stooping to wash feet or when he was submitting to crucifixion.

Hard times make us humble, and humility makes us stronger. Consider this command that Jesus gave his disciples after he humbled himself before them by washing their feet:

Now that I, your Lord and Teacher, have washed your feet, you also should wash one another's feet. I have set you an example that you should do as I have done for you. Very truly I tell you, no servant is greater than his master, nor is a messenger greater than the one who sent him. Now that you know these things, you will be blessed if you do them. (vv. 14–17)

What Jesus taught and what Jesus modeled are true for us. When we embrace the way of humility rather than resist it, we are blessed—content, fulfilled, and whole. God didn't bring you this far for you to fail. Hold his hand in your season of humility, for your good and his glory.

TESTIMONY

How Your Scars Tell Your Story

The greater the obstacle, the more glory in over-
coming it.

Molière, *L'Étourdi ou Les Contretemps*

Children show scars like medals. Lovers use them
as secrets to reveal. A scar is what happens when
the word is made flesh.

Leonard Cohen, *The Favorite Game*

Newsflash: boys are proud of their scars. Both males
and females accumulate scars over the years, especially in childhood. The difference is that boys not
only boast about their scars, they remember with perfect

clarity every detail of the injury that left them with each indelible mark. They will not only tell you the story but also remove appropriate clothing in the retelling of how they got their scar.

I have a few scars that are attached to interesting stories. One of them is on my lower right kneecap and it dates back to about 1984. I had a big crush on a girl in my class named Angie. So did all the other boys, because she was breathtakingly beautiful. She never noticed me because I was an obnoxious twelve-year-old. But I knew what all boys know instinctively: if I could do something epic and manly, and get her to see me doing it, I would win her heart and she would be mine forever.

It so happened that she lived only a few miles from me. She rode home from school with a friend, and every afternoon about 5:15 her parents would pick her up and they would drive right by my house on their way home. I decided that I would be outside in the yard, doing something epic and manly, when they drove by. Angie would get a glimpse of the real me, and I would woo her into my love.

So I grabbed a hatchet, of course, and stood on the edge of our yard cutting limbs off trees. All girls found young lumberjacks irresistible. I knew that when Angie drove by, she would see me wielding that hatchet and she'd finally understand what a strong and brawny guy I was. Soon, I saw their car coming down the road. I looked away from the limb I was hacking so I could be sure to make eye contact with Angie (a very important part of the wooing process), and right as she drove by, I raised the hatchet high with both hands and brought it down with enough force to remove the limb in a single blow in front of her very eyes. Of course, the hatchet

62

not only separated the limb from the tree but continued on its path of destruction, all the way into my kneecap.

I lost the girl. But after a trip to the ER and some stitches, what I was left with was a humiliating story and a cool scar. Angie didn't fall for me. I guess she was the squeamish type. As I've gotten older, however, that scar has served as entertainment for a dorm room full of guys, as a sermon illustration, and as a reminder of the futility of trying to impress a fifth-grade girl. Cormac McCarthy's novel *All the Pretty Horses* says it well: "Scars have the strange power to remind us that our past is real."[1]

All scars are not equal in their power to tell a story, because each one is different in the level of pain it inflicts upon us. But every scar does have a story behind it, and some of those stories need to be told. They need to be heard by other people who can find courage and hope from our stories. The proof of God's greater purpose in our pain are the scars that tell our stories of suffering. Every scar is a testimony to a trial we endured and a test that we passed.

As my friend Jonathan Martin puts it in his book *Prototype*:

> Scars are more than the sum total of tragic memories. Scars speak of identity, scars speak of calling. Scars speak of the truth of a man beneath the deception of his clothes. No wonder when Paul writes to early Christian communities, he is always speaking of the scars he has accumulated from persecution for the sake of Jesus' name. The message embedded in our scars, the code encrypted implicitly beneath ruptured skin, is not just of our pain but of God's faithfulness. Scars tell the story of who we really are and where we really come from, even when we refuse to speak the truth with our eyes or our lips. Like the rings on the interior of a

tree, everything you could ever want to know about a person can be read from their scars. . . . When nothing else in my life (including my words) rings true, then I can always rely on my scars to tell the truth.[2]

Testimony Equals Telling Your Story

When I point to that scar on my kneecap today and tell my sons the story behind it, I am literally giving a testimony of what happened, recounting the events that led to the bloody trip to the hospital. Much in the same way that I've given testimony here to my injury, we all have the same opportunity to testify to how God has sustained us and changed us through weakness and hardship. This is what Paul did with his trials. He turned them into his testimony. Read his words again:

> Three times I pleaded with the Lord to take it away from me. But he said to me, "My grace is sufficient for you, for my power is made perfect in weakness." *Therefore I will boast all the more gladly about my weaknesses*, so that Christ's power may rest on me. (2 Cor. 12:8–9, emphasis added)

Paul learned to leverage his weakness to find God's strength. The things that *hurt* him became a source of *help* for him and for others. He actually began to boast about bad things that accomplished good things in his life.

How does that work? Is it really possible to brag to other people about the hardest experiences of our lives? Can we leverage the things that have hurt us the most in order to help others who are also hurting? Moreover, can we find any redemptive purpose in the hard times we go through? The answer is a resounding *yes*! We can indeed turn our greatest trials into our greatest testimonies. And we can tell our stories of finding strength in the storm with assurance that God will use those stories to provide strength for

> *The wind and the waves that capsize us*
> *in our storms may be the same power*
> *that carries us safely to shore.*

others in their own storms. The wind and the waves that capsize us in our storms may be the same power that carries us safely to shore.

This is the definition of a testimony. It's simply our stories, complete with the good, the bad, and the ugly. These become the sources of our boasting and bragging because they are the instruments God is using in our lives to perform the miracle of transforming us into the image of Christ. God will leverage the most difficult things we've ever gone through for his own purposes. While we're enduring what feels like an endless, hopeless season, God sees the future and knows that our current test is our future testimony, and we will boast in God's power one day when we share our stories with those who desperately need to hear them. But we have to take a risk. We have to become vulnerable. We have to be willing to actually tell our stories.

Ministry Equals Story

When my mom died, I spent the loneliest night of my life in a hotel room at the Toronto airport. Without access to a private jet or a teleportation device, there was no possible way for me to get home until the next day. My tears came in waves, like little tsunamis of grief that pushed me down and held me under waves of sadness. I was drowning. Then my phone rang. When I saw who it was, I automatically knew I had to take the call. It was Perry.

Perry and I met when I was seventeen years old. We became fast friends. We understood each other and always had a good time together. But he had gone through something I'd never experienced. His mom died when he was just twelve years old. It was the single most painful part of his life. He talked about it openly, but he tried not to dwell there. Christ had changed his life as an older teenager, and he moved on from grief and depression and began pursuing God's call on his life for ministry. But the pain of burying his mom as a sixth grader had stayed with him for almost thirty years.

He'd found out that my mom had died suddenly and that I was stuck in Canada alone. He reached out to me in a way that few others could; he reached out in *empathy*. He could relate to my sense of shock and surprise. He had walked through that dark valley of the shadow of death. He could speak my language of sadness. He had passed through that valley and had passed the test, the same test I was taking. He ministered to me by being vulnerable with me. He told his story.

"Clayton, Sharie told me about your mom. I am so sorry. That's the worst thing ever. I don't have any answers for you, and I don't have any magic words to make you feel better. But what I can do is tell you that I know how you feel. I've been there. And I can testify that somehow God will get you through this. And I'll walk with you through this because I know how hard it is to feel all alone when your mom dies," he said.

Then for the next fifteen minutes he talked about his mom. How much he loved her. How she died. How cancer slowly consumed her body. How he still can't go into a hospital without having an anxiety attack. How his dad struggled after she died. He just kept talking, and I couldn't stop listening. He was speaking to the brokenness in my heart and his words were soothing. Nothing was fixed or repaired. My mom was still dead and I was still devastated. But just knowing that someone else had already been there and made it out gave me the courage to press on through that terrible night in Toronto.

Perry had suffered. And he had survived. Maybe I could too. What he did for me wasn't rocket science. He simply told his story. He showed me his scar. And at that moment a story was the only thing that could give me strength to survive the storm. His ministry to me was his willingness to share his story with me. Your hardest story is your greatest ministry.

Eric Liddell, the Olympic runner on whom the movie *Chariots of Fire* was based, said, "Circumstances may appear to wreck our lives and God's plans, but God is not helpless among the ruins."[3] When you feel like your life is in ruins, look around and realize that God is there with you. He can leverage the bad things for good, and he can do it through your story of grace and redemption. And then it's not just in us, in our suffering, that the presence of God is so powerful—it is powerful through us *for others*. When we have come through our own ruins, or even while we are still in them, God is able to use our stories to bring comfort to others.

No wonder Paul calls the church the body of Christ. This is not just a clever metaphor. Rather, when Jesus ascended, he sent the Holy Spirit so that our bodies would literally become his body, our touch become his touch, and our presence become his presence. So many people spend their lives trying to chase down the presence of God in some floating, abstract way, when in reality the main way God is present in the world is through his people, by his Spirit. Since the Spirit of God is within us, when we are willing to sit with someone else in their own pain and hurt, that is no small thing. Especially when we make our own stories of weakness a resource for others and are willing to enter fully into their suffering with them.

/////////

Canadian philosopher and theologian Jean Vanier embodies this idea as well as anyone in our time. Now eighty-five years old, this gentle giant as a young man founded the L'Arche communities, in which able-bodied persons live in small homes with severely mentally and physically disabled persons. This began as an experiment in which Vanier himself lived with a couple of severely disabled persons, and L'Arche has now become a movement that spans the globe.

One of the things that most marks Vanier's work is his understanding, from years of working with people whom society cannot and should not try to "fix," that the need to play the hero for the people around us is actually what often keeps us from being fully present in the ways they need us to be. "We are not called by God to do extraordinary things," Vanier says, "but to do ordinary things with extraordinary love."[4] And as Vanier has demonstrated over and over again through the stories he tells of working with the mentally disabled, when we sit with someone else in their own pain and suffering, we ultimately become the ones who receive the gift of grace.

One of the people who was most shaped by Vanier's powerful vision of community was the priest Henri Nouwen, who ultimately gave up a prestigious teaching post at Harvard to live with a severely handicapped man named Adam. Many of Nouwen's books chronicle the extraordinary stories of how God met him in his own areas of pain and loneliness as he made his life available to others. Over and over again, Nouwen testifies to the power at work in us when we are willing to bring our story into the suffering of another human being without reserve. We testify to the power of God to sustain us. We have the opportunity to be the same kind of friend to someone else that Perry was for me. This is the kind of friend Henri Nouwen describes so eloquently in his book *Out of Solitude*:

> When we honestly ask ourselves which persons in our lives mean the most to us, we often find that it is those who, instead of giving advice, solutions, or cures, have chosen rather to share our pain and touch our wounds with a warm and tender hand. The friend who can be silent with us in a moment of despair or confusion, who can stay with us in an hour of grief and bereavement, who can tolerate not knowing, not curing, not healing and face with us the reality of our powerlessness, that is a friend who cares.[5]

Nouwen never found this kind of life to be easy, and it will not be so for us.

Compassion is hard because it requires the inner disposition to go with others to places where they are weak, vulnerable, lonely, and broken. But this is not our spontaneous response to suffering. What we desire most is to do away with suffering by fleeing from it or finding a quick cure for it.[6]

Scars tell our stories. They connect us back to a painful thing that left a mark on us. They connect us to other people who have scars of their own. They're a testimony that we got hurt and we lived through it. And somehow, mysteriously, the Spirit of God heals us when we make our own scars available for the healing of others. "By his wounds we are healed," the prophet Isaiah says (Isa. 53:5), and as he did through the cross of Jesus, God is still using the wounds of

> *Scars tell our stories. They connect us back to a painful thing that left a mark on us. They connect us to other people who have scars of their own.*

his people to bring his healing to the world. Isn't it interesting that after his own resurrection, Jesus himself bore the scars of the cross? And he made no attempt to hide them. In fact, he showcased them, revealed them, and invited others to look at them and to stretch out their hands to feel them. They were real. They proved something. They told a story of weakness, death, resurrection, and restoration.

Bedtime Stories

I hope you were blessed to have grown up in a home where someone told you stories before you fell asleep at night. My dad was a master at this fine art. I would get out of the bathtub. Mom would brush my hair with the towel still wrapped around my shoulders. I would find the brightly colored toothpaste tube and squeeze out enough to drip down the side of my toothbrush. After brushing my teeth, I would sprint as fast as my damp little feet could carry me, out the bathroom door and down the hall and then a sharp left into the place where monsters lived under the bed and battles were fought against vampires and werewolves. My bedroom was a magical and frightening place.

I donned underwear first, then pajamas. Both items of bedtime clothing were decorated with scenes of epic super-heroes. Spiderman Underoos with the Green Goblin tied helplessly in a spiderweb cocoon. Footie Batman pajamas plastered with vignettes of the Joker locked in handcuffs and the Penguin backed against the wall by the Batmobile. Then Mama (as I called her) tucked me in tight. I reminded her to push the covers down around my neck and under my shoulder blades, as if to keep the cold and the ghosts out of my blankets. Then she tagged out and Daddy tagged in. He was larger than life and not the least bit intimidated by the evil forces that lurked in my closet. He came into my room, not to kiss me or to sing to me or even to pray for me, but to tell me stories.

My dad, Joe Elmer King, was a storytelling pro. I never knew from one night to the next if the story would center around how he and I had single-handedly defeated British general Cornwallis and three hundred redcoats in Cowpens or how we had fought off an attack from the Fishman as we were scuba diving in the Everglades. Every night he told me a story was a master class in how to give a testimony.

As a father, he instinctively knew that every little boy felt powerless and afraid against the unseen fears under his bed in the darkness. And like all good fathers, he understood that an explanation wouldn't defeat the fear. You can't reason with someone who is afraid. You have to step into the fear with them. And tell a story.

All the stories he told were filled with courage. Like the time we boarded a pirate ship and set all the slaves free. Or the time we fought back all the martians that had invaded our little South Carolina town. Or how we protected America from the Nazis who tried to invade Charleston during WWII. The man was absolutely brilliant! He knew that faith replaces fear, but not without a fight. Each story had a crisis. Each epic tale had a villain. And every night, he and I were called upon to enter the fray and draw our swords against a foe that was significantly bigger and stronger than we were. We overcame our fears when we began to fight.

Daddy took me to a place of hope with his stories. My mind took a journey to a better time and a better place where I didn't need to be scared of the boogeyman in the hall. I was standing shoulder to shoulder with my dad as we defeated one foe after another: Frankenstein, Lex Luthor, Dracula. Why should I be afraid of the dark when I could listen to a story of defeating hordes of zombies in another world?

He would talk, and I would hang on his every word. Then I would fall fast asleep. This happened hundreds of times. I was emptied of fear and filled with faith. I would feel so strong when he was done. No foe could stop me and my daddy when we were together. Isn't this precisely what you need when you're overwhelmed with weakness? You're not looking for an explanation of the nonexistence of ghosts. You need someone to tell you that you can defeat those ghosts.

A theology textbook won't get you through six weeks of chemo treatments. And a reasonable explanation of the psychological effects of betrayal are of little help when you're going through a divorce. You want someone to come to you, reach out to you, and tell you a story that lifts you above the fear and gives you hope that you can overcome what overwhelms you.

You need someone who understands the side effects of chemo to tell you their story. It doesn't even have to have a happy ending. It just has to be honest. You need someone who's suffered through the heartbreak of a divorce to simply say, "I've been there too, and somehow I made it. So will you." You don't need them to give you easy answers. You need them to be vulnerable and tell you their story.

When we suffer, our stories of survival become a source of strength. When we're afraid, a story can lift us up out of the pit of fear and transport us to a distant place filled with hope and possibility. This isn't self-help nonsense. This is the very essence of the gospel. This is how our greatest trials become our greatest testimonies!

It is not that our testimonies, our stories, will make us powerful enough to "fix" anyone else. Only God has the capacity to heal. As it was with my friend Perry, there will very rarely be words wise enough or smart enough to bring any kind of quick healing. But there is a way in which God uses us powerfully in the healing process, simply through the gift of our own stories.

Fear, Faith, and the Fight

One of the phrases I frequently use when I preach has recently become the battle cry of my life: faith replaces fear, but not without a fight. When we're afflicted with fear, the fear won't magically vaporize and disappear. It has to be evicted and thrown out.

The reason is simple; when something hurts us it leaves a mark, an emotional scar, if you will. And as long as we have the memory of that painful thing, we will subconsciously fear that same thing happening to us again. It's similar to being involved in a car crash. When you're blindsided by another

> *Faith replaces fear, but not without a fight.*
> *When we're afflicted with fear, the fear*
> *won't magically vaporize and disappear.*
> *It has to be evicted and thrown out.*

vehicle, you have flashbacks to that moment when you were hit. It makes you jumpy and nervous at intersections. When I had my first bad wreck, at age fifteen, it took me about a month to even get behind the wheel of a car again. I was followed by the fear that another wreck was lurking at the next red light.

The only way to move forward past our fear is to face the fear head-on. I couldn't run away from my fear of getting in another car accident. I had to turn directly into it. I had to climb into the car, buckle the seat belt, place my hands at ten and two, and drive again. I had to regain faith in myself. I had to prove to myself that I could operate a motor vehicle even after a nearly fatal accident. That was no easy task. Facing our fear never is. It's always a fight to replace fear with faith, because fear loves to move in and take over. Like I said, fear won't leave on its own. It has to be evicted, and it takes a fight to get it out of our lives.

Now let's go back to the power of a testimony, specifically in the bedtime stories that parents tell their kids. The real thing happening there is not that little kids pretend to be superheroes who save the day. The more powerful thing taking place is the universal battle to get the upper hand over the fears that consume and control us.

Just think about the underwear and the pajamas I described. Kids love to role-play and pretend that they are someone else, someone who is smarter or braver or stronger than their real selves. They wish they were more courageous, and somehow they connect to the characters on their pajamas when they're little. As little kids each of us wanted to be strong, but we felt weak because we were so . . . little. We felt bigger and stronger when we lost ourselves in the stories of our heroes, who overcame impossible odds and emerged victorious over the bad guys.

That's the power of testimony. We have the ability, through our vulnerability, to inspire and encourage others. That's why Paul could declare that he had entered into a new place where he was able to boast in the hard things he'd endured. He had lived a story worth telling. He had a story that others could lose themselves in, a story of hard-won hope that was available to anyone and everyone who had ever known adversity. He had experienced an intimacy with God during the hard days that he would have never known if all his days had been easy. Because he'd been comforted by God in his affliction, he wanted to share that comfort with others in their affliction.

He said as much in the first part of his second letter to his friends in Corinth, with keen insight into the power of sharing in the suffering of others.

> Blessed be the God and Father of our Lord Jesus Christ, the Father of mercies and the God of all consolation, *who consoles us in all our affliction, so that we may be able to console those who are in any affliction*, with the consolation with which we ourselves are consoled by God. (2 Cor. 1:3–4 NRSV, emphasis added)

According to Paul, we don't have to waste our weakness. We can leverage it for the benefit of others who are limping along with the same struggles we have endured. That affliction you're going through today can be used for good tomorrow, so resist the urge to try to hustle through it as quickly as possible. God may be leaving you in that rough spot for the sake of another person on down the road who will need to hear your story of survival, redemption, and victory. Or he may be allowing you to face a trying situation so that the people who observe your trial will see a clear picture of what a true Christian is.

The Extra Mile Equals the Testimony Mile

As a guy who's always been fascinated with history, I find myself spending copious amounts of time reading boring old books or watching documentaries on PBS about the Civil War, British colonialism, or the adventures of Lewis and Clark. But my favorite period in history, by far, is the rise and fall of the Roman Empire, particularly during the life of Jesus.

In college I picked up a book by Will Durant called *Caesar and Christ* that opened my eyes to just how powerful the Romans really were and, more surprisingly, how powerful the movement of Christianity was in that it eventually grew to supplant the power of the caesars. Books like this one, as well as *Jesus and Empire* by Richard Horsley, helped me understand the hostile world Jesus was born into and the impossible odds the earliest Christians faced when they began testifying to pagans, Greeks, Romans, and Jews that Jesus was truly the Son of God and the Savior of the world.

The Romans created a brutal empire that conquered other nations, states, and people groups at will. They imposed their imperial cult as they built roads throughout the ancient world and spread their culture for thousands of miles. When they would invade a land, they would set up a Roman outpost of authority, usually consisting of a governor (Pontius Pilate, who ruled ancient Palestine, was one such governor) and a police force. The job of the soldiers was to keep the *Pax Romana*, which was Latin for "the peace of Rome." Caesar, who claimed to be picked by the gods as a sort of ruling deity, gave orders to his provincial officials throughout the empire. They carried out his orders through the power of the Roman army, complete with battle-hardened soldiers who had little concern for the lands they occupied or the people they ruled over.

These Roman police forces acted with impunity throughout the empire. They could do just about anything they wanted so long as it was in the service of keeping the *Pax Romana*. These Roman "peacekeepers" were funded and fed by Rome itself, but Rome took that money from the very countries it invaded in the form of taxes and tribute. The taxes they collected were unfair, exorbitant, and crippling to almost everyone forced to pay them. But there was no way to stand against this abuse. There was no appeal process. You paid whatever tax Rome demanded.

In Matthew's account of the Sermon on the Mount, we read that Jesus said some things that were revolutionary to his listeners for the very fact that he was teaching in Galilee. This region was the training ground for Jewish nationalists who hated the Roman occupiers and plotted their removal from Israel. They were called zealots because of their love for the nation of Israel and their radical commitment to seeing the holy land rid of the pagan occupiers, in order for the temple to be rebuilt in Jerusalem and the glory of God to return to his people. To say they hated the Romans wouldn't come close to describing the animosity that existed in the hearts of the people who were listening to Jesus teach that day in Galilee.

Caesar had appointed a puppet king named Herod, who is famous for his amazing building projects (the Temple Mount and Masada are two examples) as well as his insecurities and manic fits of murderous rage (he slaughtered members of his own family in paranoia that they were plotting to overthrow him). One of his sons was ruling Israel when Jesus preached these words, and Jewish nationalism was at a fevered pitch.

Jesus said something in this context that stopped the crowd dead in their tracks. The comment was made in reference to the occupying Roman (Gentile, pagan, unwanted, despised) powers. "If anyone forces you to go one mile, go with them two miles" (Matt. 5:41).

Scandalous! Unheard of! Jesus was clearly referring to a particular Roman law that allowed any Roman soldier to stop a Jew on the road and compel him or her to drop what they were carrying in order to assist the Roman soldier in bearing his load. Of course, the soldier could simply make the Jew carry his load out of laziness or a power trip. However, the law only required the Israelites to walk one mile for the soldiers. Not two. Only one. So Jesus tells his listeners to go beyond obligation.

The second mile is not an obligation. It's an opportunity. The extra mile is our witness to the world. It's the way Jesus expected his followers to win over Roman soldiers to the kingdom of God, and it's still the way we win an unbelieving world to Christ. It's how we testify to a lost world that Jesus has made a difference in us. When we are forced into hard situations that are beyond our control, we can become bitter or we can become *better*—better witnesses to God's greatest power.

No one paid attention when a Jew carried a heavy bag of grain for a Roman soldier for one mile. The first mile was an obligation. But imagine the scene when a soldier tells a

---

The second mile is not an obligation. It's an opportunity. The extra mile is our witness to the world.

Jew he's fulfilled his duty and can drop the bag, but he tells the Roman that he wants to keep on carrying it for him! Now he has everyone's attention, including the soldier's. The second mile was an opportunity. The second mile gives us a story worth telling. We quit too quickly. We want to get by with the absolute minimum. We bail out after our obligation is completed. In looking for the easiest path we fail to develop the muscle and the endurance for the second mile, and we miss the opportunity that most often lies in doing the difficult thing and denying our own right to an easier road.

The point of the second mile was to show the Romans that the Jews were different from them. They did not demand, they offered. They did not compel, they invited. The children of Israel were operating from a different worldview, one of simplicity and virtue found in the God of Scripture. The Romans operated from a worldview of power, conquest, and greed. Roman hearts could be won, one at a time, by simple acts of radical service that went contrary to the expectation. Freedom would come not from a Jewish uprising or revolt but from the internal liberty of being free to serve your enemy, testifying to the transforming power of God in a person's soul.

The only way for good to win over evil is to go beyond obligation. The second mile in our lives makes the "Roman" world ask why we would go the extra distance under such a heavy burden. The second mile opens up conversations that would never happen in the first mile. The second mile makes us better humans and better Christians. It builds the muscle we need to carry the gospel and the endurance we need to remain faithful through the hardest seasons of life. The second mile makes us feel weak, but it's really making us stronger. It's our greatest witness to the world. What feels like a trial and looks like a test is quickly transformed into a testimony as we walk the extra mile. People may not agree with our politics. They may even be skeptical of our religious convictions. But they cannot argue with our stories.

Rick Warren has said that your greatest ministry will come out of your greatest hurt, and he should know. As a pastor, he's built a small congregation in Orange County, California, into a powerful global movement. As an author, he's written *The Purpose Driven Life*, which stands as one of the most widely read nonfiction books in modern history. As a leader, he's prayed at presidential inaugurations and consulted heads of state from Africa to Latin America. But as a man, he's endured perhaps the most painful ordeal a father could ever go through: the death of a child.

He has shared publicly how his son's ongoing battle with mental illness and eventual suicide shaped and formed him as a husband and pastor, making him more tender and understanding overall—but specifically, it has enabled him to leverage his platform on behalf of the millions of Americans who

> *What feels like a trial and looks like a test is quickly transformed into a testimony as we walk the extra mile.*

also suffer from mental illness. Rick and his wife, Kay, are now telling their story and using their influence as advocates for those wrestling with mental illness. His greatest ministry may not ultimately be building a megachurch or selling millions of books. It may be this telling of his son's story that gives other parents, spouses, sisters, and brothers the courage to seek help for the person they love who is fighting for their mind . . . and their life.

Your current trial is your future testimony, so don't hesitate to tell your story. Who knows how many people are just waiting to hear what you have to say? How many will connect the stories of their own scars to your story of survival when you show them yours? Your scars tell your story and your story is a testimony to God's power that's revealed in your weakness.

PRESENCE

No One Gets an Exemption, but You Do Get a Companion

"Because he loves me," says the LORD, "I will rescue him; I will protect him, for he acknowledges my name. He will call on me, and I will answer him; *I will be with him in trouble*, I will deliver him and honor him."

Psalm 91:14–15, emphasis added

We convince by our presence.

Walt Whitman,
"Song of the Open Road"

Let me ask you a pretty straightforward question. Don't overthink it. Just respond honestly from your gut: Would you rather go through life completely alone and never experience hard times, or would you prefer to go through seasons of difficulty and weakness with someone you loved by your side? I can simplify the question this way: Would you rather have an exemption *from* hard times or a companion *in* hard times?

Now I can't read your mind and I'm certainly no clairvoyant, but my instinct tells me that if you really thought long and hard about these two options, you'd come to a conclusion similar to mine. I believe it's actually preferable to have a companion stand beside me during my greatest struggles than to be immune from all difficulty but never know the tender, faithful love of a friend.

The importance of presence really cannot be underestimated. Paul spoke of this when he stated, "But he said to me, 'My grace is sufficient for you, for my power is made

---

What gives hope to the one in trouble is not just the protection *of God. It's the* presence *of God. His presence is your protection.*

---

perfect in weakness.' Therefore I will boast all the more gladly about my weaknesses, so that Christ's power may rest on me" (2 Cor. 12:9). Evidently, when we are at our weakest, God's presence is strongest. His power rests on us in a special way when our weakness is undeniable and tangible.

This is the essence of the passage from Psalm 91 quoted above. Read it again. God is making promises to the person writing these words, and these are good and comforting promises. The writer finds himself in trouble, so he calls on God to rescue him, and God promises to give him protection, to deliver him, and to honor him. But as I read these verses a few times, what I noticed was surprising. What gives hope to the one in trouble is not just the *protection* of God. It's the *presence* of God. His presence is your protection. Everything hangs on seven simple words: *I will be with him in trouble.*

Presence Brings Peace

When I was a boy, I experienced this in a way that left a deep impression on me. Just about everything good that I know or that I am, I learned from my dad. He was an entirely different kind of man. Born at the beginning of World War II, he lived in crippling poverty that would render our modern-day family powerless. People in general were much tougher and more resourceful in that time, not to mention simpler in their daily needs, but my father lived in a home without electricity or running water. His family grew or slaughtered all their food, except for the occasional bag of sugar or salt from the general store, and even when they bought items they seldom paid with cash. They traded eggs or milk or butter from the farm. I've always wished that I could have lived in that day and that I could have known my dad then and been his friend. I think we would have been the closest of companions.

Our close relationship was built on a foundation that my dad laid early on. We did things together; we worked in the yard, we cultivated a garden, we worked on cars. We played together; he came to my practices and ball games, took me hunting, told me stories, and threw the football after work in the front yard. It was during one of our father-son adventures that I first understood peace in the midst of panic.

One of the most vivid memories I have of my father involves a scouting trip we made in preparation for deer season. We always checked the woods to find out where we should hunt. That year we saw a lot of tracks and sign, so much in fact that we lost track of where we were going. We just kept walking, amazed at how many deer were in the area, until my dad suddenly froze as we walked along a small ridge above a creek bed.

He leaned against an oak tree. He looked left. Then right. Even from behind, I could tell something was wrong. Then he turned slowly in a complete circle and surveyed the surroundings. My heart began to pound. I felt light-headed all of a sudden. I wiped my brow, which had become sweaty in a matter of seconds—when I realized my dad was afraid.

"Son, I think we're lost," he said. That was it. Then he set out briskly. I understood that I was to follow him.

I realized that in all the years we had been in the woods together, I had never seen this area, and I doubted that he had ever been there either. But that wasn't what scared me. What scared me was the realization that my dad was scared. I had never seen him frightened of anything, ever, in any situation. I wasn't sure how afraid he was, but I was absolutely terrified. We crossed a small creek and pushed straight up a steep ridge. He was trying to find a high spot from which he could get a better look. By the time we reached the top of the ridge, my clothes were soaked with sweat. He turned to face me.

"Well, son, I don't know where we're at," he said. "I lost track of the trail when we were looking at those tracks, and then when I realized I was lost, I thought I knew the way back to the truck. But all these little pine trees got me turned around, and I think we need to pray and ask God to help us get back to the truck before it gets dark."

As the sun gracefully descended below the trees, the air grew colder and the woods darkened. My mind began seeing things in the trees just beyond us. I started crying. I was breathing hard and my heart was racing. My sweaty clothes had turned ice cold and clung uncomfortably to my body. We didn't have any food or water. My mouth was as dry as a desert. And our only flashlight had exhausted its batteries. Things seemed grim. My father hadn't spoken in an eternity. I was waiting, hoping, begging God to make my dad say something to give me some hope. I just needed to hear a word from him. Then finally . . .

"The gravel road ought to be up here in just a minute," he said.

I was too consumed with fear to even watch where we were going until I followed Daddy through a line of bushes. I watched him take a big step off of a steep bank and I heard the crunch of gravel under his feet. Then I jumped! Both boots landed with a thud, and I stumbled and fell on a thousand small stones, never happier to be anywhere in my life. My dad helped me up, wrapped his arms around me, and squeezed. His warmth pushed against my cold, clammy arms. "Thank you, Jesus," he whispered as he held me close. That gravel road would take us to the truck and the truck would take us home. We were literally "out of the woods," and soon we were sitting side by side in his old Ford truck.

That's how we like our stories: a crisis, some drama, and then a happy ending. Everything works out and everyone lives happily ever after. But in the middle of a hard time, we question if we will ever find any resolution. So the only thing we have to cling to, when the sun goes down and shadows fill the woods with frightening images, is trusting that God is present. We believe he is there beside us. We follow him, even when he doesn't speak for a while. We just keep moving, right behind him, in his footsteps, trusting that he will get us out of the woods and get us home. There's no guarantee how long it will take or how far we will have to journey. The only guarantee we get is a faithful companion in the darkness who promises not to leave us or abandon us. And that companion is better than an exemption. No matter how dark it might get, God is always present whether we feel him or not.

Darkness Brings Distortion

Darkness in the woods brings on fears that don't exist in the daytime. When the light is plenteous, you can see everything as it really is. A pine tree stump. A big granite rock on the side of a creek. The top of a dead poplar tree covered in briars. But when the sun goes down, your eyes see things that aren't there. The stump becomes a giant black bear. The rock becomes a rabid wolf. The dead poplar becomes a family of hungry cougars.

Darkness is a distortion. When we can't see what God is up to, we create images and shapes that frighten us. Harmless, inanimate objects turn into wild enemies that wait to tear us apart.

And even though there are only two natural fears that all humans possess, the fear of loud noises and the fear of falling, our view becomes distorted when it turns dark. An appointment with the doctor distorts into certain cancer in your mind. An email from a superior asking to meet distorts into certain unemployment. A text from your spouse asking if you can talk tonight distorts into a major conflict and a big fight before you even get home.

When the light goes completely out and it's total darkness, we imagine ever more frightening scenarios that put us in peril. The peril makes us panic. When we can't get an answer to our prayer, or a breakthrough in the relationship,

---

Darkness is a distortion. When we can't see what God is up to, we create images and shapes that frighten us.

---

or a good report from the doctor, or a raise from our boss . . . we assume that everything will be bad from here on in. What we forget in those moments is the one thing we need most: God's presence. He has not left us alone in our darkness. He is there. It's as simple as calling out to him in the dark.

When my dad leveled with me about how lost we were, I felt a combination of panic and peace. I was frightened at the thought of being alone in those big woods after dark, at only ten years old, with the possibility of being eaten alive by any number of wild animals that lurked in the shadows or freezing to death. But alongside the sense of panic was a quiet, subtle sense of peace. I was not alone. I was with my dad. Everything was going to be ok as long as I was with him. I just knew it. I believed it. His presence was the source of my peace.

Over and over in my adult life, I have felt those two conflicting emotions at the exact same moment. I panic at the least little thing. When our checking account gets low or when one of my boys gets a headache, I immediately fall to pieces inside, assuming the worst possible scenario. But I also know that we will somehow have enough money this month to pay the bills and that the small headache is not a brain tumor, it is just a kid who needs to go to bed a bit earlier. And though it seems impossible that fear and faith can dwell in the same vessel at the same time and take up the same space, they coexist all the time.

As a matter of fact, fear must be present for faith to exist at all. Fear is the thing that calls faith out of us. The obstacle that's too big for us, the situation we can't fix, the sickness we can't cure—these bring fear to the surface. But

Faith does not mean the absence of fear. Faith means moving forward in the face of fear.

if we look behind those fears, we will find that faith is hot on their heels. Every fear is an opportunity to have faith in God's power. Faith comes before the miracle. Proof comes after the miracle. So I pray for faith, then I wait for proof.

Fear is actually a kind of faith; it's faith in the wrong thing, the bad thing, the worst thing. We succumb to fear when we forget that God is still there with us, in us, and for us.

I think we have gotten the idea of faith all wrong. Faith does not mean the absence of fear. Faith means moving forward in the face of fear. It's owning our fear and forging ahead into an uncertain outcome. It's refusing to feed our fears and facing them instead. God brings peace in the moment of panic as if out of nowhere, perhaps from a dark and quiet corner of our hearts that we haven't heard from in a while. But right there, just in time, when we need it most, while the sky is falling and the bills keep coming and dark clouds keep gathering, peace comes. Faith wins out.

God promises his presence in times of pain. Furthermore, I believe that God's presence is actually magnified in our weakest moments, when we feel most helpless and in need of a companion to stand by our side. God will be with us in trouble. With *you*! What an amazing promise. It's an even better reality when it happens, and it happens in lots of ways:

1. A verse from the Bible that speaks to you in a special way early one morning when you can't sleep.

2. A friend who sends you an encouraging text message right before you walk into a meeting you've been dreading for days.

3. A hug from your husband right before you feel like you're going to break down from the weight of your to-do list.

4. Something your pastor says in his sermon that is exactly what you needed to hear to help you through something you're struggling with.

5. A phone call from your mom or dad just to check on you to see how you're doing.

What we all need most is not an *exemption* from hard times. That would be a boring, lonely life. What we crave deep down in our hearts is the presence of a *companion* who walks with us through whatever we have to endure. God himself promises to be that companion, and he also sends us lots of other people as his little ambassadors to hold our hands and lift us up when it feels like the wheels are coming off our lives.

There's a powerful example from the life of Paul that proves how God can send others to pick us up from our pit and gather around us when we feel like we can't go on.

> Then some Jews came from Antioch and Iconium and won the crowd over. They stoned Paul and dragged him outside the city, thinking he was dead. *But after the disciples had gathered around him,* he got up and went back into the city. The next day he and Barnabas left for Derbe. (Acts 14:19–20, emphasis added)

Unbelievable! Paul, who himself had instigated the stoning of Stephen, was now the recipient of this horrible form of death, but as he lay on the ground, evidently dead, his brothers gathered around him. Was it their prayers that saved him? Was it their presence that healed him? Was it the power of their companionship that lifted him up from the point of death? Yes, yes, and yes! God used his other disciples to bring Paul back from the brink. No one survived a stoning, much less walked back into the same city where he had incited a riot, unless there was a supernatural strength present through the presence of friends. How amazing . . . the stoning made Paul stronger. *God doesn't promise a free pass from hard times; he promises his presence. And his presence is the most powerful kind of protection we could ever have.*

Panic and Peace

I've learned that I'm capable of feeling two conflicting emotions at exactly the same time (and I'm not a middle schooler—

I'm a grown man with a beard). It seems like the life I am living throws so many things at me at once that I can't keep up with it all. Do you ever feel like this? Maybe a better question would be, do you ever *not* feel like this? So we find ourselves torn between *freaking out* over circumstances that are way outside of our ability to control and *trusting God* to somehow come through for us. There's the reality of how hard things can be, and there's the hope that eventually the season will pass and things will get better. My grandmother used to say to me, "You know why they say 'And it came to pass'? Because it didn't come to stay. It came to pass, and this too shall pass."

I've decided that I live somewhere between the extremes of panic and peace. Yep, that's my home these days. I moved in there about fifteen years ago and have been there ever since. And yes, there are days when I live more in the place called panic.

- I have a book deadline that I can't possibly meet.
- Our ministry is growing and we need to hire two more employees, but there's no money in the budget for extra salaries.
- I sense that a friend is angry or offended at something I've done, and I can't stop thinking about it.
- A close friend just told me that his wife is leaving him.
- There's a confrontation I've put off for weeks staring me in the face.
- I didn't sleep well last night, and I'm about to leave home for two days to preach. Oh yeah, and I'm late for my flight.

- I get a call from the doctor telling me my dad has decided to stop dialysis and will die in a few days. That call comes in when I'm on vacation with my family, our first family vacation in eighteen months.

Then there are days when I live more in the place called peace. The weather is perfect outside (70, sunny, and dry). My kids haven't argued with my wife all day. I had a good night's rest. My back doesn't hurt. I went to the gym, read my Bible, and ate healthy food for lunch. No one in my extended family died or had to have major surgery.

But we both know there are very few perfect days. The average day is a blend of both panic and peace.

- The doctor bill is simply outrageous and you can't pay it . . . but they agreed to reduce the charges and not turn you over to a collection agency.
- The transmission in the car is completely shot and it's going to cost $860 to fix . . . but a friend at church said he could do it for $300.
- The college you always dreamed of attending accepted you but you can't afford the tuition . . . but you have another option to take classes at a local community college or even take classes online.
- Your mom was just diagnosed with breast cancer . . . but they think they caught it early enough and the doctors say she should be ok.

We can spend all our time trying to avoid the panic and all our energy trying to find the peace, but the real world is a strange and dizzying combination of the two. Right in the midst of a day that was actually going pretty good, the sky can turn black and three horrible things can pop up out of nowhere in fifteen minutes. Conversely, in the middle of a near nervous breakdown after a stressful conference call, a bad exam, or a toddler's meltdown, you can sense the tangible presence of God begin to calm you down and sustain you. Panic and peace are strange bedfellows, indeed, but our lives bear witness that God is right there in the moments when these two worlds collide in our hearts.

A companion in hard times is far superior to an exemption from hard times. John Newton said, "For the believer, a prison with the Lord's presence is a palace, and a palace without the Lord's presence is a prison."[1] His presence is part of the greater purpose in our trials.

Perspective on Presence

If I may, I would like to ask you that question again, the one from the beginning of the chapter: Would you prefer an exemption from all the struggles you will go through in your life, or would you prefer a companion to walk with you through those hard times?

For nearly thirty years, I remembered with great clarity that afternoon I spent lost with my dad in the Sumter National Forest. I've told the story at churches and universities and big events with thousands of people in the crowd. When my own two boys were old enough to go in the woods with me, I told them the story, about how scared I was, how I just kept following my dad until we made it out to the gravel road. All those years, I thought that story was for me. It helped me when I was afraid. It brought peace in times of depression and joy in times of discouragement. My dad and I would often remember that day when we were together later on in his life, especially at Christmas or Thanksgiving when the family gathered around the table. As a matter of fact, I think it was one of his best memories, judging from the frequency with which he told it.

It wasn't until the final days of his life that my eyes were opened to another perspective on the day we got lost together. As I watched my dad get sicker and weaker, I knew that his death was not just inevitable; it was imminent. When he became so weak that he could no longer walk by himself or even hold a cup, I knew the end of his earthly life was right around the corner, and I was sucker punched by the fear of what it would be like for me to live in a world without my dad's presence.

He was always there. He never left us. He came home from work at the same time every night. He attended all of my games. He was the most constant human presence I'd ever known, and the doctors were telling me to get his affairs in order and prepare myself for his death. I began waking up in the middle of the night with panic attacks, the result of dreams in which I was preaching his funeral or I was in the hospital room when he passed away. And almost every time I would wake to the crushing weight of another nightmare in which my dad died, I would then automatically revert back to that ten-year-old boy following his daddy in the dark through the woods, trusting in his presence and believing we would make it out of there. That memory comforted me in ways that words can't adequately convey.

During the last few days of his life, I stayed by his side in the hospital. We were able to talk. And pray. I brushed his hair and shaved his face. I rubbed his feet and his arms. I held his hand. One evening as I read the newspaper by his side, he started weeping and sobbing. This wasn't out of the ordinary. The medication he was on, coupled with the reality that he would live only a few days without dialysis, made him extremely emotional. He reached over and stuck out his hand in my direction. I met his hand with mine, and we held hands like we had when I was a little boy. Like we had done so many times in my life.

"Son, do you know what I was just thinking about?" he asked.

"No, Daddy, why don't you tell me? Was it something bad or something good?" I responded.

He composed himself enough to speak, between sobs. "I was remembering that day you and I went scouting down to Sumter National Forest. The day I got us lost in the woods down there."

Was he feeling guilty for putting me through something traumatic at such a young age? I wanted to console him.

"Daddy," I said, "it wasn't your fault that we got lost. You know that I was never angry with you for that. We just got turned around in the woods, that's all. And you got us out of there safe and sound."

"Clayton, I want you to know that I have always loved you, and I have always loved being with you," he said. "When I think about that day we got lost, I don't remember so much how afraid I was. I just remember you and me being together. That's all that really matters in life, son. And I'm so glad that you are still right here with me, as I get ready to die and be with the Lord. Just remembering how God got us out of those woods that day gives me the strength to know that he will get me out of here safe and sound and home where I belong. I'm glad you're still with me."

It was impossible for me to hold back the tears as I typed his words at my kitchen table on a Sunday afternoon. I cried because I still remember. I remember the ensuing panic that engulfed a scared little boy, but what carries me through hard times is the memory of the presence of my dad. In his dying moments, what also carried him through was the presence of a person whom he needed most—me. He remembered the same panic and the same peace I recalled. I was with him and he was with me. A boy with his daddy. Holding hands and crying together. Filled with pain. Surrounded by grief. Overcome with years of suffering. Tested to the breaking point. Staring eternity square in the face. Wondering when the end would come.

But right there at my dad's deathbed, in the face of pain and panic, all the fear in the world couldn't compare to the tender moment of peace we felt in each other's presence. And just hours later, he was gone. That story wasn't just for me. It was for him too. It carried him straight into the presence of God.

Nobody Gets an Exemption

That's what our pain does for us. It invites God into our story. It invokes his presence in a special way. Pain *clarifies* what really matters and *simplifies* what outlasts temporary turmoil. Long after the hard thing has come and gone, we will have the memory of God's friendship. Years after the suffering has ended and the crisis has passed, we will be telling the story of how God made us stronger when we were weaker than we'd ever been. And decades after we are dead and gone from this life, our stories of God's faithful presence will live on, inspiring others to reach out in the darkness and take God's hand in theirs. They may even tell our stories to their children. Or in a book.

If we all got an exemption from hard times, we would have no stories to tell and nothing of substance to hold on to. We could never encourage another living soul to press on through hard times. We could never speak the tender, vulnerable words, "I know what you're going through. I've been there, and you are going to make it." Each of us will know the bitter taste

> *If we all got an exemption from hard times, we would have no stories to tell and nothing of substance to hold on to.*

of loss, the deep ache of grief, and the heart-racing panic of fear. It's inevitable and unavoidable. So we might as well stop wishing for an exemption and start enjoying the presence of our Companion. In hard times, we must embrace the fear we're feeling while listening in faith to what God is saying: *I am with you, I am in you, and I am for you.*

A companion is far superior to an exemption. Reach out and take his hand. Follow him. He knows the way out.

> Yes, my soul, find rest in God;
> my hope comes from him.

Truly he is my rock and my salvation;
    he is my fortress, I will not be shaken.
My salvation and my honor depend on God;
    he is my mighty rock, my refuge.
Trust in him at all times, you people;
    pour out your hearts to him,
        for God is our refuge. (Ps. 62:5–8)

STRENGTH

Weaker than Water, Stronger than Spiderman

All that is gold does not glitter,
Not all those who wander are lost;
The old that is strong does not wither,
Deep roots are not reached by the frost.
From the ashes a fire shall be woken,
A light from the shadows shall spring;
Renewed shall be blade that was broken,
The crownless again shall be king.

J. R. R. Tolkien,
The Fellowship of the Ring

The world breaks every one and afterward many are strong at the broken places.

Ernest Hemingway, *A Farewell to Arms*

Where does strength come from?" Jacob was four years old when he asked me that question. He was our first child, so we were learning things about children for the first time, especially the different stages a little boy goes through as he's growing up. Around the time he turned four, he embarked on the stage called "I am a little boy who thinks he's a dinosaur, a superhero, and a monster, and I will scream at everyone and intimidate them by flexing my muscles." (I'm pretty sure that's a real stage, by the way.)

Thus the question. He wanted to know how he could get more strength, I assume, so that he could feel bigger than he actually was. He was becoming aware of how much bigger other people were than him. He had begun making comments about how he wanted to be big like me one day. So he began projecting himself in ways that made him feel larger and stronger. He would roam around the house growling like an angry pit bull at inanimate objects. He would roar at random people in restaurants. He would climb up on stage at events where I was preaching and unleash a bloodcurdling scream while he flexed his muscles like a bodybuilder, face bloodred and eyes bulging. The more people laughed and applauded, the more he showed off his strength.

"Where does strength come from, Daddy?" What a great question. In the purity of my son's desire to understand the source of strength lay a reflection of our own frailty and our desire to overcome it. From the mouths of babes, as they say.

I gave the obvious answer that any parent would give. Strength comes from eating healthy food, like oatmeal and bananas and spinach. Strength comes from playing and exercising and being outside and drinking lots of water. Strength comes from getting plenty of rest and going to bed early (when your parents say it's bedtime). But as I was telling him all these ways he could be strong, I sensed the Holy Spirit whispering to me deep in my soul. I was leaving out the most essential element. My answer wasn't wrong, but I was forgetting the true source of real strength. So I saved the most important part for last, not as an addendum but as the big finish.

"Jacob, you don't prove that you're strong by breaking things or making loud sounds. You show how strong you are by letting others go first, by sharing, and by loving people and being kind to them. And son, real strength doesn't come from food or exercise or rest. It comes from God." As the words came out of my mouth, I choked on them. I knew that this was true, yet I still struggled to believe it, to submit to it, to live by it. I needed to practice what I was preaching because the last thing I felt was strong. Inside I felt as weak as water.

Jacob's simple and wise response to me? "Yeah, Daddy, I know it. Where else would strength come from? God made the whole world. He's the strongest person in the universe. Even stronger than Spiderman."

The Strength of a Child

In the world's terms, the strongest ones have the most power and influence. Yet one of the beautiful ironies of the kingdom of God is that children—the weak and powerless—are the most blessed. In fact, Jesus taught that we have to become as children in order to enter the kingdom. The kingdom won't allow us to get by on the strength of our ego or on our rugged Western individualism, or allow us to posture or pretend to be tougher than we are. We have to be willing to embrace the small, almost naïve trust of a child to experience the strength of God in all of its fullness. I learned this the hard way.

My dad tried to remain living at home after my mom died, but he was too sick. He needed round-the-clock care, so we moved him to an assisted living facility. It was a ninety-minute drive one way from my house to see him. While his basic needs, such as food and medication, were taken care of by the staff there, his emotional needs seemed to grow more acute by the day. He was living in a room all alone. His wife was gone, I lived in another state, and his bipolar disorder became more acute as his health declined.

I tried my best to see him every week. We talked on the phone daily, but most of our conversations were one-sided; I would ask him questions and he would give one-word responses. I would tell him about Sharie and his two grandsons, and then I would give him an update on where I had traveled recently and how my ministry was going. He was so sick that he could barely hold his head up. Eventually he couldn't even hold the phone up to his ear for more than about thirty seconds. He would always ask me to come see him, but he would follow up that request with a caveat. "I know how busy you are, son, and I don't expect you to come down here to see a sick old man. I just miss you, and I think about you all the time. I don't have anything else to think about. I just sit here by myself all day. Seeing you and your family is the only thing I have to look forward to anymore."

It's utterly impossible to convey how my heart split in half every time he said that to me. And he said it every time we talked. Every single time. I knew how much it meant to him to have visitors. He had originally refused to move to an assisted living facility closer to me because he wanted to stay close to his house, in hopes that he would get better and be able to return home. I gave up on any attempt to convince him that he was too sick to ever go back and live by himself. But he never went back home. When he finally admitted that the doctors were right, it was too late for him to move to North Carolina with us. He was physically too far gone. So I traveled a well-worn path to Clinton, South Carolina, to take him pictures of our kids or just to give him a shave or rub diabetic cream on his feet so that they wouldn't have to start amputating his toes.

Each trip to see my father became more difficult, with the foreboding sense that each time I left I may never see him again. Imagine what it feels like to say your final goodbyes with your father over and over again, never knowing if he would live another twenty-four hours. It tore my heart to shreds. I would cry all the way there. I would compose myself

---

Each trip to see my father became more difficult, with the foreboding sense that each time I left I may never see him again.

---

in the parking lot while praying out loud for God to help me pull myself together before I went inside. I would force myself to go in and spend half a day in his room without falling all to pieces, and then cry all the way back home. I did this for eight months. That drive kept getting longer and my heart kept breaking.

As my father neared the end of his life, I was overcome with a paternal instinct to get my two boys in front of their grandfather as many times as possible before he died. I wanted them to have conversations with him, to have memories of Papa Joe (as they called him), and to own at least a small sliver of a relationship with the man who had loved me so faithfully my entire life. I felt like the diabetes and heart disease were robbing my children of the blessing of knowing my father. And what a tragedy that they would never know the joys of fishing with him, hearing his stories, or sitting beside him in church as he belted out the words to "How Great Thou Art" along with the choir. I couldn't give them the things that a grandpa could give to his grandsons, and I was painfully aware of that reality. But I could get them in a room with him while he still had breath in his lungs.

So at every opportunity, I would juggle school, sports, and my travel schedule to load up my boys for a trip to the nursing home. At first the environment frightened them. The home was filled with older adults, many with advanced Alzheimer's. They would call out to people who weren't there, scream out in pain, accuse staff members of trying to abduct them, and even wander into my dad's room occasionally. Some would stare off into space like they were waiting on a visitor who would never come. Others would just slip out when the nurses weren't looking. It scared my kids to death when the cops were called in one day because a man in his nineties had escaped and the staff couldn't find him. The facility went into total lockdown, and my kids freaked out. The cops eventually found him outside hiding in the bushes.

And then there was the circus that erupted each time I would walk through the front door of the nursing home with my boys. At ages six and nine, they became the center of attention in a home full of old people who relished the memories of their own children and grandkids. Every resident there wanted to talk to them, hold their hand, ask them questions, or invite them to sit on their lap. So my boys didn't exactly love going to see my dad.

On one particular visit on a bitterly cold day in February, I learned another lesson about real strength. By this point, my dad wasn't having any more good days. There were only varying degrees of bad days. But I pressed on nonetheless. We were going to surprise him. I had learned not to call him before I visited because the anticipation of seeing me would create such anxiety in his mind that when I arrived he would be a basket case. Time was subjective to his deteriorated mind, partially because of his pain medication. It was better to show up unannounced. The first time I popped in for a "surprise" visit he commented that he felt more joy than he did as a little boy on Christmas morning. I wanted to leverage that element of surprise to bring him a few more moments of joy before he died.

As I drove through sheets of rain with my boys in the backseat, I really hoped he would be happy to see them. But there was no guarantee. It turned out to be a worst-case scenario when we finally got there. He had fallen again and scraped his knee on the floor. They had a hard time controlling the bleeding because of the blood thinner he took daily to keep his heart working. And to top it all off, he had been vomiting since the previous day when he returned from dialysis. We walked into an emotional minefield.

I felt so sorry for my dad. He was simply pitiful. He'd lost so much weight. He couldn't eat much of anything, and when he did it was a chore to keep it down. The worst part?

The sight of my boys and our big surprise visit barely even brought a smile to his face. He was just too weak and too sick to experience joy. And as I was trying to get the boys to tell him about school and basketball, he began having a panic attack. These were frightening episodes in which he lost all control of his emotions and would cry and scream for several minutes. I took the boys out to the lobby. I went back in to check on my dad, and he'd lost control of his bowels and bladder while I was out of the room. He looked up from his chair directly at me and sobbed, "I don't know why God doesn't just take me home. This isn't a life. I wish I were dead."

I got down on my knees and wrapped my arms around him. We cried together. It was the only thing I knew to do. I recalled how, as a little boy, he would hold me tight in his arms and comfort me when I was afraid or upset. Now the

---

He looked up from his chair directly at me and sobbed, "I don't know why God doesn't just take me home. This isn't a life. I wish I were dead."

---

roles had been reversed. I was loving him in the same way that he had always loved me. I was a reflection of my dad's tenderness and care. He had nurtured me, and in his last days on earth I was privileged to nurture him.

The wonderful nurses came in a few moments later and helped clean him up, but he told them that he wanted me to shave him. After they left, I brushed his hair and gave him a close shave. As I was wiping the shaving cream off his neck, he said, "Son, I am so sorry that you've had to see me like this. I never meant for you to have to take care of me like a little baby. I'm supposed to take care of you. Please forgive me. I didn't take good care of my health. When I die, will you tell Jacob and Joseph that I'm sorry I didn't live long enough to see them grow up? It's all my fault that they won't have a grandpa."

That was almost too much for me to handle. All I could manage to say was, "Daddy, don't worry about that. The boys know that you love them." He responded by asking me, "Will you promise to tell them stories about me? Will you tell them what a good daddy I was and what a good time you and I had together when you were growing up?" It was like he was saying his final farewell to me. I wondered if he had a premonition that he would die that night. I fetched my boys from the lobby and brought them into his room to say goodbye. We gathered around his chair and all three of us laid our hands on his shoulders and prayed for him. My boys asked Jesus to help him rest that night and to not be sad. We all hugged and kissed him, and then we headed to the parking lot.

Up until that moment, this was the hardest day of my life. It was more difficult than the day my mother died, because when she passed I knew that at least I still had my dad with me. But this day was much more gut-wrenching because I honestly believed it would be the last time my boys would see their grandpa. And the last time I would see my father.

As we left, my boys hopped into the backseat, put on their headphones, and popped a movie into the DVD player. I sat alone in the front seat. Within a mile of the nursing home, the emotional tidal wave I had been holding back all day finally crashed into me. Tears exploded from my eyes. Waves of grief crested over me, and I sobbed and struggled to breathe. The rain was still falling outside. Then it let up. Then it started again. It was a mirror image of what I was going through inside the car. Tears and sobs. A few moments of calm. Then another wave of grief like another sheet of rain. I had cried before, but never like this.

The saving grace in all of this was that Jacob and Joseph were immersed in their movie in the backseat and were immune to the weight of sadness that had settled down hard

---

I swallowed hard and tried to pull it together, but it was hopeless. The grief was an unstoppable force. It was like trying to stop a freight train.

---

on my shoulders. I didn't want my kids to see me like that. It would scare them. I swallowed hard and tried to pull it together, but it was hopeless. The grief was an unstoppable force. It was like trying to stop a freight train.

But I had to pull it together! I was driving the boys straight to basketball practice at the YMCA. As soon as I walked in, people would wonder what was wrong with me. Even worse, they would ask, and I would try to answer then fall all to pieces again, embarrassing myself and my kids. As we got closer to the gym, I prayed harder and harder for God to somehow, miraculously, give me the strength to get out of that car and walk into that building with my boys to basketball practice. But it wasn't working. I just kept crying. Ugly, uncontrollable crying.

We pulled into the parking lot. I would tell the boys to go in without me. I would sit in the car as long as it took me to compose myself. It was the weakest, most helpless feeling I'd ever known. As we parked, the boys took off their headphones. Then something truly wonderful happened. They immediately observed my frail state. I was broken and they knew it. Nowhere to go. No way to hide. I was unprotected and vulnerable in front of the two little boys that I'd been trying to be strong for.

Jacob spoke up. "Joseph, Daddy is really upset. His heart is broken because his daddy is dying. Let's lay our hands on Daddy and pray for him like we prayed for Papa Joe, and let's ask God to give Daddy the strength he needs." Then my children leaned forward. Jacob placed both hands on my left shoulder. Joseph placed both hands on my right shoulder. And they began to pray for me. Out loud.

///////

What happened there in my Honda Pilot was nothing short of miraculous. God was touching me through the hands of my children. As they prayed with their tiny hands on my shoulders, the weight that had been sitting there lifted off and floated away. I felt like angels were standing with them, defending me, protecting me, and surrounding me. My weakness was replaced with strength. I felt it fill me up. I imagined an empty glass pitcher. That was what I felt like. Then I imagined water being poured into it, rising to the top, filling it until it overflowed. That was my heart. That was me. Weakness being displaced by strength—strength to carry on, to get out of the car and walk into basketball practice, to make it one more day. God was empowering me.

His strength was *actually* being made perfect in my weakness. Instead of just reading about it, I experienced it personally.

I wish I could tell you that I've been strong ever since that frigid afternoon in the YMCA parking lot. That would be awesome, wouldn't it, if ever since that moment I've had reserves of strength that I could call on whenever I needed them? If it were only that easy. But that's not how it works. In the same way that my body converts carbs and proteins into energy when I need it, God gives me his strength when I'm weak and need it. But I have to eat to get that energy. You have to be willing to consume what God is willing to distribute. You don't *achieve* strength. You *receive* strength.

My children were God's gift of grace to me. They were his chosen vessels, his administration of the strength that I needed, the strength I certainly did not possess, not even to turn off my car and unbuckle my seat belt.

Upside-Down Strength

This whole book stands on the premise that the darkest and most profound difficulties of our lives are used by God to make us stronger. This all sounds good enough—until you are, in fact, in a broken place. Emotionally, spiritually, physically, psychologically—you may have never felt more bankrupt, as if every ounce of your soul is spent. It's especially problematic if you buy into larger cultural assumptions about what it means to be strong—to keep your cool, keep your composure. Don't let your knees buckle under the weight of the burden you carry. Put on your toughest face, act like you've got it together even if you know deep down you are coming apart. Don't let anyone or anything hurt you.

I have found these ideas to be especially prevalent among men, given a daily dose of the message that to be strong is to appear tough at all times. It's a terrible way to think about masculinity. But of course there are women who have had the same kind of terrible expectations assigned to them—to never let their feelings show, for that is a sign of weakness. If that kind of absolute composure is your idea of strength, the gospel will not help you become strong at all. In fact, each of these cultural assumptions about strength is antithetical to what we learn in the New Testament about strength— they are the polar opposite of how strength is defined in the kingdom of God.

The primary subject of Jesus's own teaching is the kingdom of God—not some mythical, faraway place, but the reality of living under God's reign right where we are. The kingdom of God is present here and now wherever and whenever people love and serve Jesus. That's the ultimate realization of the prayer Jesus gave us: "your kingdom come, your will be done, on earth as it is in heaven" (Matt. 6:10). That prayer is being realized slowly, piece by piece, all across the globe as people allow the love of Jesus to be revealed where they live. But this kingdom is very different from the kingdoms of this world. It is in the world but not "of the world." It does not originate within this world. It is counterintuitive and countercultural. The kingdoms of the world are established through displays of dominance, through wealth and weapons, through status and success. The kingdoms of the world are established through sheer force.

But when Jesus inaugurated the kingdom of God, he inverted this kind of strength, and he turned the old ways of thinking about strength and power upside down. In his famous Sermon on the Mount, the manifesto of the kingdom, Jesus announced those whom God has called blessed. To put it mildly, it is a shocking, subversive list:

> Blessed are the poor in spirit,
>> for theirs is the kingdom of heaven.
> Blessed are those who mourn,
>> for they will be comforted.
> Blessed are the meek,
>> for they will inherit the earth.
> Blessed are those who hunger and thirst for
>> righteousness,
>> for they will be filled.
> Blessed are the merciful,
>> for they will be shown mercy.
> Blessed are the pure in heart,
>> for they will see God.
> Blessed are the peacemakers,
>> for they will be called children of God.
> Blessed are those who are persecuted because of
>> righteousness,
>> for theirs is the kingdom of heaven.
> Blessed are you when people insult you, persecute you and falsely say all kinds of evil against you because of me. Rejoice and be glad, because great is your reward in heaven, for in the same way they persecuted the prophets who were before you. (Matt. 5:3–12)

It is an upside-down list, the opposite of any and every kind of person that the world in its present order would call blessed. The world says that the attractive, the influential, the mighty, and the victorious are the blessed ones. Jesus says those who weep, those who are brokenhearted, those who are gentle, and those who are hurting are the ones who are blessed in God's kingdom.

They are not blessed simply because they are hurting, as if there is something intrinsically good about suffering—as we saw before, God never wants us to suffer for suffering's sake. *The things that break us are the things that bring us closer to God. They seem to get his attention.* The broken, the bruised, and the marginalized—these are the people who don't have the option of living under illusions of strength in the ways that so many in the world do. They don't live in denial. Their wounds have robbed them of any human pretensions of strength.

The truth is, even at our best and brightest, no one is really able to sustain themselves. We are in desperate need of God and of each other, and that is true even when our circumstances seem most ideal. It is our weakness that allows us to

---

So shake off the pretense. Stop managing your image. Learn to care about only what God says about you!

---

see ourselves as we truly are: small, needy, and dependent. Weakness doesn't exactly make us need God or others more; it just makes us aware of the need that's already there—that is always there.

Thus, in the kingdom of God, being strong doesn't mean we never fail, never stumble, or never get sliced up. In fact, it is within the rule and reign of Jesus that we are able to own our weaknesses. And in a mysterious way, as we courageously face down the fears that threaten to swallow us whole, we really are getting stronger. So shake off the pretense. Stop managing your image. Learn to care about only what God says about you!

The Crucified God

This is never on display any more clearly than in the cross of Jesus. The cross is certainly an odd example of strength—especially since Jesus hardly went hopping and skipping onto it. The Gospels record how Jesus himself spent the night before his crucifixion in unspeakable agony, allowing the anguish of his soul to spill to the ground through his tears and blood. He pleaded with his Father, "If it is possible, may this cup be taken from me" (Matt. 26:39). He did not accept the cross without angst, but he did ultimately accept it: "Yet not as I will, but as you will" (v. 39). That is precisely the kind of people the kingdom of God produces—those who are able to embrace their pain rather than live in denial of it. We're not robots. Neither was Jesus. Pain actually hurts us, as it did him.

It is not just in the anguish of the garden that we find God's strength. In Christian theology, the cross is how God fogives sin and wins over evil—the principalities and powers in the natural and supernatural order that seemed to be running the show through base human displays of power. It is not *despite* the suffering Jesus endured on the cross but precisely *because* of it that Jesus reigns victorious. "And having disarmed the powers and authorities, he made a public spectacle of them, triumphing over them by the cross" (Col. 2:15). The things that we endure will make us strong, but not in the ways the world tells us to be strong. There will be a strength and comfort that come from God's Spirit as we, like Jesus, embrace the terrible reality of the crosses that lie before us with total trust in God's grace to make us stronger.

Remember my son Jacob's question: Where does strength come from? Strength comes from God alone, the crucified God, the One with ultimate power to raise Jesus from the dead. Strength comes from the cross. Both the cross of Jesus, where God has already accomplished his victory over the forces of evil, and through our own crosses, which are allowing us to be conformed to the image of Jesus.

As John Stott writes in his masterpiece *The Cross of Christ*:

> We turn back to that lonely figure in the Gethsemane olive orchard—prostrate, sweating, overwhelmed with grief and dread, begging if possible to be spared the drinking of the cup. From his agony of dread, as he contemplated the implications of his coming death, Jesus emerged with serene and resolute confidence.[1]

When it seemed like darkness had won, when it looked like Jesus was finished, when there seemed to be no possible way . . . the crucified God became the resurrected Lord and Savior of the world. When you feel like you can't make it another day, when all your reserves are tapped out, when you think you're going crazy and things will never turn around, remember Jesus. He is alive. And he is with you, in you, and for you.

Like my two seemingly weak children gave me strength through their humble prayers, God makes us stronger through weakness: a desperate prayer in the garden and a despicable death on the cross. We gain strength in knowing just how strong Jesus really is—even stronger than Spiderman.

// **6**

REGRET

A Murderer, a Martyr, and a Metamorphosis

Brothers and sisters, I do not consider myself yet to have taken hold of it. But one thing I do: *Forgetting what is behind* and straining toward what is ahead, I press on toward the goal to win the prize for which God has called me heavenward in Christ Jesus.

Philippians 3:13–14, emphasis added

We cannot live our lives constantly looking back, listening back, lest we be turned to pillars of longing and regret, but to live without listening at all is to live deaf to the fullness of the music.

Frederick Buechner, *The Sacred Journey*

A few years ago, I had a hard conversation with an old friend while standing in the lobby of his church. I had just preached the Sunday morning message and was standing out front shaking hands and signing books. I watched him hover outside the perimeter of people, evidently waiting until the crowd had dispersed so he could speak with me privately. As I suspected, as the last person walked away he approached me at last. We embraced as brothers. I hadn't seen him in over a year. He had just returned from his third tour of duty during our wars in Iraq and Afghanistan. He was married to a lovely woman. They had a beautiful child. And he had just gotten his orders for his fourth tour of duty. He told me he would be shipping back out soon, too soon, to serve his country by doing what he was trained to do.

He was struggling with leaving his wife and child again. He was also wrestling with how to square up his faith in Jesus with his particular job in the military. He wondered how he could reconcile the call to love his enemies as a Christian with his training to stop murderous men before they took more lives. On top of that, he was suffering the effects of post-traumatic stress disorder, a result of the carnage he had witnessed and the stress he had endured on his previous tours. "Clayton, I need your prayers and maybe your advice," he said. "I'm not in a good place right now. I'm really anxious all the time. I don't sleep more than a few hours at night. I've been to counseling for PTSD. And now I have to get ready to head back over there again. I just don't know if I can do it."

We stood there for a long time. I asked questions to try to keep him talking. I was his friend, but in that moment I was also a pastor to him. As I probed deeper into what was at the root of his depression and fear, he dropped the bomb on me. "Well, I didn't want to talk about it, but the real thing that's got me so torn up isn't so much the time away from my family. It's the regret I carry that's killing me."

I knew he was a soldier and I assumed he'd seen blood and carnage, but I was completely unprepared when he really opened up and became totally vulnerable. Up until that point I wasn't aware of exactly what he did in the military. He was a sharpshooter, a military assassin. He told me he was trained to "stake them out and take them out." He was trained not to miss.

"I've killed people, Clayton, and I don't mean in major combat or a big firefight. I stalk one bad guy at a time. I watch him for days, and then when we know for certain he's a murderer or a terrorist, they give me the order and I take him out. I'm one of the best, but I see their faces all the time after I take them out. I can't live with the guilt anymore. Can God ever forgive me? Can anything good come out of what I've done? What should I do with this regret?"

What would you tell someone if they asked you that sort of thing? I wasn't prepared to field a question of such serious consequence. Even though I was guilty of all sorts of sins and shortcomings, I found it difficult to relate to someone who had pulled the trigger that released the bullet that took a human life. I did the best I could to point him to Scripture and God's mercy. I put my hand on his shoulder. We bowed our heads and prayed together, asking God to somehow redeem his regret. There was no easy answer for him. There never is an easy answer when it comes to living with regret.

When You Can't Go Back

There's one thing in my life that still follows me around, and I have to fight the tendency to allow it to control me. It's my greatest regret: *I wasn't with my dad when he died. He died alone. And sometimes I hate myself for that.*

My father had been at the nursing home for eight months, and they would transport him to dialysis three days a week. On a Wednesday, he had another heart attack during dialysis and was too weak to undergo another surgery. His doctor called me, then handed the phone to my dad. His words are still fresh to me.

"Son, I just can't do it anymore. I can't take another surgery. I'm tired of fighting. I'm ready to be with Jesus. I miss your mama. I'm ready to go home. Can you come stay with me until I die?" Even writing those words unlocks a vault of grief deep in my soul, because I remember exactly where I was and what I was doing when he asked me to come stay with him until he died.

I was at the beach with my family. We were going to play miniature golf. We hadn't had a family vacation in eighteen months. Taking care of Dad had become our first and only priority since Mom died. We had been at the beach for two days when we packed up our bags and drove six hours to the hospital. It was the longest drive of my life. I cried the whole way. When we arrived at the hospital, friends and family members were there. As soon as Daddy saw me, he burst into tears and held out both arms for me. I got to him as fast as I could. I buried my head into his hair and kissed his face and his cheeks.

Eventually everyone left, including my wife and boys. It was just the two of us. I stayed with him in that room for two days and nights. I slept beside his bed and rubbed his arms and feet. I shaved him, combed his hair, and fed him a few bites of Jell-O. Then on Friday morning they moved him from the hospital to a hospice facility where he would be until the end came. I helped get him into his room at hospice, filled out the papers, and prayed with him. He'd become listless from the pain medication but wasn't suffering any physical pain. The doctor said he may live another few days.

Sharie and the boys had been in a hotel since we arrived at the hospital. I didn't expect them to stay at hospice with me. And my sons, Jacob and Joseph, had their baseball awards banquet that night back home in North Carolina, an hour away. I wanted them to go to their awards banquet. I had a choice to make. I could go with them and leave my dad there in the care of the hospice staff. He wasn't in pain. He was essentially unconscious by the time they got him settled in. And I would be back in no time.

Or I could stay with my dad another night and miss being with my boys on their special night. I specifically thought how horrible I would feel if I left and he died alone while I was gone. But my family had sacrificed so much the past eighteen months, we had cut our vacation short to be with my dad, and I didn't want to miss another big moment with my kids, so I decided to risk it. He was sleeping, so I slipped out of his room without saying goodbye, thinking he wouldn't even know I was gone. I would be back in a few hours anyway. Right after the awards banquet.

And he died while I was gone. My bad dream had come true. Again. The banquet started late and lasted forever. By the time we got home, I was so exhausted that I feared falling asleep at the wheel if I tried to drive another hour back to hospice. A six-hour drive back from the beach and two sleepless nights in the hospital with Dad had wiped me out. I just needed a few hours of sleep in my own bed. I decided I would get up at 5:30 the next morning and drive down and stay with him until he died.

The phone rang at 5:20 a.m., but it wasn't my alarm. It was the nurse at hospice telling me my dad was close to the end. Twenty minutes later, as my family piled into the Honda Pilot, trying to make it in time to say our last goodbyes, the phone rang again. He was dead.

I stood in my driveway with hot tears dripping off my chin and nose. He was gone, and I hadn't been there when he died. My mom hadn't been there because she was dead. I hadn't been there because . . . I was TIRED? Really? How pathetic. I immediately hated myself. Why did I take the risk

I knew as long as I lived, I would carry that regret of not being by my dad's side and holding his hand while he died.

of going to the banquet? Why did I leave his side? Why didn't I make some strong coffee, suck it up, and go to him? I had never known real regret until that moment. I knew better, but I made the wrong choice. And now it was too late. I could never change what I had done. I knew as long as I lived, I would carry that regret of not being by my dad's side and holding his hand while he died.

I preached my father's funeral on Father's Day. The whole time I was talking about what a great man he was, on the inside I was secretly beating myself up for abandoning him.

Some of the tears I shed that day were from my grief. Some were from my regret for not being there in his last moments. For a long time after he died, I internalized my self-loathing and refused to tell anyone. It was stealing my joy and eating me alive, until I eventually broke down and told my wife. I couldn't hold it in any longer.

"How could I leave my dad like that? What was I thinking? He died alone, and I should have been there. I will never be able to forgive myself!" It was that moment of vulnerability that I believe opened my heart to God's redemption of my regret. He used my wife's words to do it.

"Clayton, your dad wasn't alone when he died. Your dad was never alone. That man loved Jesus more than anyone we've ever known, and Jesus was in him and with him when he took his last breath. Do you honestly think your father, in heaven right now with the Lord, is angry or disappointed with you? Really? No, your dad is fully healed in the presence of God. He's proud of you and he loves you. You didn't fail your dad. Give that regret to God. It's too heavy for you to carry."

In that moment, I decided to lay down that heavy burden at the feet of Christ. I felt the weight lift off of me when I realized my dad was in the presence of pure joy, fully redeemed. Do I still regret not being there? Yes. But knowing that Jesus was there to redeem my father and take him home is greater than my regret. When the regret comes back, I have to remember that my dad is redeemed.

Regret and Redemption

If we formed a support group for people who live with heavy burdens of regret, the apostle Paul would probably be qualified to facilitate that group. Upon his conversion to the Christian faith, he had to walk a long and hard road of receiving God's forgiveness for his past deeds. This also meant learning to forgive himself for the terrible sins he'd committed in the name of God. *Especially the sin of murder.* There is no better example I can think of than Paul to show you how God can redeem your regrets. By understanding who Paul was and what he did before he became a follower of Jesus, we can better know what he meant when he said that God's strength is made perfect in our weakness.

Just as my friend in the military had stalked out those considered "bad guys" and had "taken them out," so Paul had deliberately targeted certain people for the sole purpose of putting an end to their evil ways. We can read one account of this in the book of Acts. This story gives us the context we need to see the backstory of how Saul became Paul and how he saw God's greatest power revealed through his weakness.

His name was originally Saul, just like Israel's inaugural king. He was a professional Jewish attorney and religious expert. He came from the right bloodline and had an unparalleled pedigree. He was a rising star among his peers. He'd made a name for himself among the Hebrews as being zealous for a pure Judaism, one not stained by so-called Jews who were convinced the Messiah had already come in the person of Jesus of Nazareth. Saul and the system of Judaism categorically rejected all claims of these new "Christians" who believed Jesus had been raised from the dead after his crucifixion. But as more and more Jews converted to faith in Jesus, this rigid religious system, which governed every aspect of life among the Jews, began to crack and crumble.

The Pharisees, the Sadducees, and the Sanhedrin feared losing their control over their people, and much like they had plotted the demise of Jesus, they planned to put an end to this growing movement led by his followers. This was the context into which Saul emerged. He boasted all the accolades of a true Pharisee, but he took it to the next level. Saul wouldn't stand by while impostors hijacked his religion. He embarked on a crusade to round up as many Christians as he could by arresting them.

One of his arrests would prove to be a defining moment in his life that would produce both his greatest regret and his redemption. He brought to trial a young man named Stephen, who had been chosen as both a servant and a leader among the Christians living in Jerusalem. Luke, who tells us about Stephen in Acts 6, called him a man who was filled with the Holy Spirit and with faith. Evidently, his character and bold faith in Jesus as the true Messiah had made him stand out to Saul, who brought him before the Sanhedrin to stand trial and be made an example of what would happen to other Christians who upset the balance of power among the Jewish religious elite.

> Now Stephen, a man full of God's grace and power, performed great wonders and signs among the people. Opposition arose, however, from members of the Synagogue of the Freedmen (as it was called)—Jews of Cyrene and Alexandria as well as the provinces of Cilicia and Asia—who began to argue with Stephen. But they could not stand up against the wisdom the Spirit gave him as he spoke. (Acts 6:8–10)

God's hand was clearly on Stephen. The more he spoke about the gospel, the more trouble he stirred up among the religious power brokers, and Saul was one of them. They came up with a plan to shut him down. It was a page straight from the same playbook they had used when they tried to stop Jesus.

> Then they secretly persuaded some men to say, "We have heard Stephen speak blasphemous words against Moses and against God." So they stirred up the people and the elders and the teachers of the law. They seized Stephen and brought him before the Sanhedrin. (vv. 11–12)

Stephen found himself standing before the high priest, answering charges of blaspheming God. Yet something surprising happened. As the authorities questioned him, he stood before them in evident weakness but spoke to them with unbelievable strength. Aware that these men had the power to put him to death, Stephen threw caution to the wind and proclaimed the gospel of Jesus Christ and his resurrection from the dead with clarity and conviction. His words sealed his fate, but without flinching, Stephen began with Abraham and traced God's story of rescue and redemption all the way to the crucifixion of Jesus, even declaring that his very accusers were guilty of murdering the Messiah. They were so furious that they dragged him from their presence and immediately began the process of executing the death penalty. Stephen found himself in the hardest place of his life. Could God reveal his greatest power in this moment of helpless weakness? Indeed he could, and he did.

Like a Rock

The angry crowd descended upon Stephen and dragged him outside the city to stone him to death, but before the first stone was cast, he had a vision: Jesus Christ, in heaven, standing at the right hand of the heavenly Father. Stephen declared out loud that in the moment of his greatest trial, Jesus was present, watching over him and preparing to welcome him into heaven upon his death at the hands of his accusers.

> But Stephen, full of the Holy Spirit, looked up to heaven and saw the glory of God, and Jesus standing at the right hand of God. "Look," he said, "I see heaven open and the Son of Man standing at the right hand of God." (7:55–56)

This is the only place in the Bible where Jesus is described as standing at the right hand of the Father. In every other instance, Christ is described as being seated. Evidently, Jesus stood up to welcome Stephen to heaven. *The first Christian martyr received a standing ovation from the Son of God.*

Then the mob hurled rocks at Stephen's face and head, splitting his skull, breaking off his teeth, and lacerating his flesh down to the bone. This angry crowd was filled with nameless people from all walks of Jewish life—except for one person who is specifically mentioned by name. "Meanwhile, the witnesses laid their coats at the feet of a young man named Saul" (v. 58).

That's curious. The mob was instigated by insecure religious professionals who feared losing control of a corrupt system. It was made up of zealous blue-collar workers and everyday Israelites who were swept into a religious frenzy by leaders who wanted to execute a blasphemer who dared to claim that Jesus was God in the flesh. Some cheered, some watched in approval, and others threw stones. But they all laid their outer garments at the feet of a young man named Saul.

This brief detail of Stephen's execution is filled with meaning. Why would Luke think to include this tiny comment as he writes the story? Actually, it mattered greatly to the future of the church and the worldwide spread of the gospel. Jewish law required that if a legal charge was to be brought

As Stephen died, Saul stood by proudly, as if he were doing God a favor. But things were not over yet. No, they were just getting started.

against someone for a crime, specifically one as serious as blaspheming God, it must be verified by witnesses. But just like our modern-day justice system, the accusation had to be brought by a plaintiff. Someone had to officially accuse Stephen of this crime, and that person was Saul. He was instigating the whole thing. How do we know Saul was responsible for Stephen's death? We see it in this small detail of the mob laying their coats down at his feet.

It was tradition that the person bringing the accusation would cast the first stone at the person found guilty of the crime. Jesus even mentions this when the Pharisees dragged a woman caught in adultery before him in the temple. As Jesus rose to her defense, he said, "Let any one of you who is without sin be the first to throw a stone at her" (John 8:7). Christ himself was well aware of this Jewish legal precedent.

That first stone was powerfully symbolic. The person who threw it would then stand back and witness the execution while the crowd finished the job that the accuser had started. And to make sure that they could properly aim the stones at the guilty party, they would slide off their cloaks and robes so their throwing motion would not be impeded. They would lay them at the feet of the one who had thrown the first rock. This was Saul. As Stephen died, Saul stood by proudly, as if he were doing God a favor. But things were not over yet. No, they were just getting started.

> While they were stoning him, Stephen prayed, "Lord Jesus, receive my spirit." Then he fell on his knees and cried out, "Lord, do not hold this sin against them." When he had said this, he fell asleep. And Saul approved of their killing him. (Acts 7:59; 8:1)

Saul singled out Stephen, brought him to trial, and accused him before the Sanhedrin. He approved of their sentence. He threw the first stone. He stood by as a witness to Stephen's death. He cheered on the angry mob as they finished him off.

But as he watched Stephen die, I believe he himself was arrested by the joy and peace emanating from the dying man. Stephen prayed to God, in the same way Jesus had prayed, to forgive the men who were murdering him. It's certain that Saul was aware of Jesus's own crucifixion and how he had prayed, "Father, forgive them, for they do not know what they are doing" (Luke 23:34). It's even likely that Saul was there that day at Golgotha, watching Jesus die and listening to his tender prayer for mercy on behalf of his killers. As Jesus died, so did Stephen. I believe this image lingered in Saul's mind for the rest of his life. The scene of this dying man, being executed because of Saul's actions, would be the catalyst for Saul's own conversion to Christianity. I believe it would also haunt him until his own death.

Forgetting What Is Behind

On the heels of his big success in stoning Stephen, young Saul pursued his ambition to make an even greater name for himself among his peers. He leveraged the momentum and headed north on his mission of stopping the spread of the Christian faith among the Jews. As a dual citizen of both Israel and Rome, Saul used his connections and was granted legal authority to travel more than one hundred miles into modern-day Syria to arrest Christians who were "deceiving Jews" in Syrian synagogues. Acts 9 paints a powerful picture of what happened next. As Saul journeyed along the road to Damascus to arrest any who belonged to "the Way" and have them deported as prisoners to Jerusalem, something—Someone—stopped him dead in his tracks.

It was Jesus Christ. Saul came face-to-face with the very person he refused to believe in.

> As he neared Damascus on his journey, suddenly a light from heaven flashed around him. He fell to the ground and heard a voice say to him, "Saul, Saul, why do you persecute me?"
>
> "Who are you, Lord?" Saul asked.
>
> "I am Jesus, whom you are persecuting," he replied. "Now get up and go into the city, and you will be told what you must do." (Acts 9:3–6)

Talk about a defining moment!

Saul no longer doubted the resurrection of Jesus from the dead. How could he at this point? Jesus was physically present in front of him, surrounded by glory and light. Saul asked him who he was and then answered his own question by calling him "Lord." Imagine what Saul must have been thinking. If Jesus really was alive, then he had surely tracked down Saul to punish him for killing Stephen and to stop him from persecuting more Christians! He was angry, and he'd come back with a vengeance, right?

Not exactly. Jesus didn't take revenge on Saul. He didn't vaporize him on the spot or strike him with leprosy. He let him live and he gave him instructions to go into Damascus. Jesus had been working on a plan. It was a pretty big one. Jesus had also appeared to a Christian man in Damascus, Ananias, who would help Saul recover from his encounter with the Lord. Notice what Jesus says to Ananias concerning Saul's future life as a Christian:

> But the Lord said to Ananias, "Go! This man is my chosen instrument to proclaim my name to the Gentiles and their kings and to the people of Israel. I will show him *how much he must suffer for my name.*" (vv. 15–16, emphasis added)

Jesus was about to take the arch nemesis of Christianity and make him its greatest ambassador. The persecutor would become a church planter. God would transform the murderer into his messenger. The one who had killed Stephen would

---

The persecutor would become a church planter. God would transform the murderer into his messenger.

---

become one who would call sinners to repentance and salvation. *But he would have to suffer.* The blessing of salvation would carry with it a burden of suffering. Saul would experience physical and emotional pain. He would see great fruit in his labors but he would suffer great loss as well. His own people would consider him a traitor. They would plot to kill him like he had plotted to kill Stephen. And as we've already seen, he would eventually suffer a similar stoning because of the gospel, and would boast in it!

> Then some Jews came from Antioch and Iconium and won the crowd over. They stoned Paul and dragged him outside the city, thinking he was dead. But after the disciples had gathered around him, he got up and went back into the city. The next day he and Barnabas left for Derbe. (14:19–20)

Don't miss this: Paul was stoned but survived, not because he was strong but because in his weakest state (the point of death) he was surrounded by friends who prayed for him. Then, miraculously, he courageously went right back into the city where the mob who tried to kill him resided. Evidently, facing death head-on and surviving makes you stronger than humanly possible. Paul even included this event in his own testimony of how many things he had suffered as a Christian at the hands of his enemies.

> I have worked much harder, been in prison more frequently, been flogged more severely, and been exposed to death again and again. Five times I received from the Jews the forty lashes minus one. Three times I was beaten with rods, *once I was pelted with stones*, three times I was shipwrecked. I spent a night and a day in the open sea. (2 Cor. 11:23–25, emphasis added)

And though he knew Stephen was in heaven, Paul would live with the regret of knowing he had taken an innocent life.

He would spend years trying to forget what he had done. You can hear the pain of past regret in his voice when he writes:

> Brothers and sisters, I do not consider myself yet to have taken hold of it. But one thing I do: *Forgetting what is behind* and straining toward what is ahead, I press on toward the goal to win the prize for which God has called me heavenward in Christ Jesus. (Phil. 3:13–14, emphasis added)

How Your Biggest Messes Can Become Your Greatest Message

We look back with regret in two ways: *I missed out* and *I messed up*. We regret the things we wish we had done. We should have spent more time with our kids, studied harder, taken better care of our health, or started following Jesus sooner. We *missed out*. We also regret the things that we shouldn't have done. We slept around, partied too much, began drinking at an early age, got caught up in the wrong crowd, or opened our big mouth. We *messed up*. But in Christ, you can be redeemed from every regret, the times you missed out and the times you messed up.

Regret is a powerful force. It can pull us under and hold us down, gasping for breath and praying we make it back to the surface. It can lie dormant for days, even months, until we forget it's there, and then at the most inopportune moment it leaps from the shadows and pounces on us like a wild animal waiting to make a kill. Regrets are anchored in our past but they live in our present and they threaten to hijack our future. They're always there, even when we think we've forgotten them, and they can jump on our back with little warning.

Regret is tied to memory. You recall a mistake you made, a hurtful word you spoke to a friend, or a terrible decision you made that caused you or someone else pain. You remember a bad relationship that your parents and friends warned you about. You kick yourself for being so stubborn and headstrong. Regret is accompanied by phrases such as:

- If I could go back in time, I would have done things differently.
- I wish I had known back then what I know now.
- I wish I had waited and thought it through.
- That was the worst decision I ever made.
- I wish I had listened to their advice.
- Why didn't I see that coming?

Regret is also tethered to the feeling of disappointment. The result you were looking for never materialized. Instead, you were left with something less than what you wanted. And the memory hurts. Regret always carries with it a form of self-criticism that is able to see things clearly in retrospect that you were blind to on the front end. This can bring about self-loathing and blame. You tell yourself repeatedly that it's your fault. You should have known better. How could you have made such a dumb decision? And the cycle becomes more and more vicious.

Moreover, regret is exasperated when you observe other people who aren't weighed down with the same heavy burden you carry. You may have a sibling or a friend with more money or a better education or a more fulfilling marriage than you have, and you struggle to be happy for them even though you know that's the correct response to their good fortune. But you can't push through the regret of knowing that if you'd made better decisions, you could have some of the joy and happiness that you imagine they have.

Or what's worse is watching someone who's made even worse choices than yours seemingly dodge all the negative fallout. Whether a result of chance circumstances, rich parents, or a corrupt system, they seem to be doing fine while you languish in the past where your life took a turn that you wish you could go back and undo. They did worse in school, they flunked more classes, they dated more losers . . . so why are they doing fine?

It's hard to live with our regrets. They are a source of discouragement. They can punch us square in the gut and knock the breath right out of us. Our regrets make us feel weak. So what do we do with them? Where do we put them? Can they be redeemed for anything good or useful? Yes! Our regrets don't have to be utterly useless. God can redeem them by using them to change us and teach us valuable lessons for the future. He allows us to share them with others as a way of helping them avoid the same mistakes we've made. Our regrets become signposts pointing to God's grace.

Our biggest messes become our greatest message when we release our regret to God's redemption. Paul's words in 2 Corinthians serve as our guide in leveraging hard times for our growth and God's glory.

> I have labored and toiled and have often gone without sleep;
> I have known hunger and thirst and have often gone without
> food; I have been cold and naked. Besides everything else,
> I face daily the pressure of my concen for all the churches.
> Who is weak, and I do not feel weak? Who is led into sin,

and I do not inwardly burn? If I must boast, I will boast of the things that show my weakness. (11:27–30)

What was driving him to say these things, beyond what we can see concerning his struggle with pride and self-sufficiency? Was there something deeper that affected him? Was there something that had wounded Paul at a more visceral level, something from his past that followed him around and haunted him relentlessly?

I believe there was. It was his greatest regret. It was the killing of Stephen. And like our regrets, *it never left, but it was leveraged.* It was a constant reminder of what he was capable of apart from the grace of God. It was a daily battle to believe that he was completely forgiven for his past sins based on God's love, not his own goodness. The death of Stephen, though tragic, served as an example of unflinching faith in the presence of persecution and pain. And for Paul, Stephen's weakness was actually how God's greatest power was revealed, because at his weakest moment God gave Stephen the strength to pray for the forgiveness of his murderers. Then God answered that prayer not only by forgiving Saul but also by changing his name and sending him out as a witness to the power of the gospel. Saul became Paul, and Paul literally changed history. He wrote nearly half of the New Testament. He allowed God to redeem his regret instead of using the source of weakness as an excuse to stay stuck in that place of shame.

Paul would never forget the stoning of Stephen. It would *scar* him, but it would also *shape* him into one of the most effective ministers of the gospel in history. His greatest regret was redeemed by God and leveraged for God's glory. He pressed on into the future because of what he'd learned from his past. And his greatest source of hardship became the very thing that pushed him closer to Jesus as his only source for purpose and joy for the rest of his life.

Do I still regret not being in the room with my father when he took his last breath? You bet I do. If I could do it over again, I would have never left his side for that baseball banquet. But what's done is done, and I can't go back and change the past. Neither can you. There's no future in the past, but there is grace when we press on toward what lies

---

There's no future in the past, but there is grace when we press on toward what lies ahead.

---

ahead. Will I ever forget what is behind me? No. I won't forget the regret of missing my dad's final moments any more than Paul could forget watching Stephen praying for the forgiveness of his murderers in the same way Jesus did. And just like God leveraged Paul's regret to bring him into a relationship with Christ, the weakness I live with concerning my greatest regret forces me to look to Christ alone for all my strength.

Did Paul regret killing Stephen? Of course. But that regret, which could have made him weak, pushed him closer to Jesus and made him stronger. The ancient church father Augustine called Saul's conversion "the violent capture of a rebel will."[1] The rabid wolf became a humble lamb. *A murderer experienced a metamorphosis through the death of a martyr.* Our current condition doesn't have to be our ultimate conclusion. What could make us weak can actually make us stronger when we lay down our regrets at the feet of the Redeemer.

VULNERABILITY

How to Open Up When You Just Want to Shut Down

He who cannot reveal himself cannot love, and he who cannot love is the most unhappy of all.

Søren Kierkegaard, *Either/Or*

The strongest love is the love that can demonstrate its fragility.

Paulo Coelho, *Eleven Minutes*

Vulnerability is not knowing victory or defeat, it's understanding the necessity of both; it's engaging. It's being all in.

Brene Brown, *Daring Greatly*

When I remember my father, the great irony that still puzzles me is what a great man he turned out to be in spite of the fact that he didn't have a father after the age of ten. Truth be told, it was the shame my dad felt as a result of his own father's abandonment that both marked him as a wounded soul and made him into a hero. I never met my father's father. He died from throat cancer, the result of years of smoking cigarettes, before my parents adopted me into their family. My dad never talked about him. Neither did my aunt and uncle, or my grandmother. Francis King was a gigantic mystery.

When I was a kid, we would visit my grandma on Sunday afternoons, and one of my childhood delights was exploring her house: her pantry, spare rooms, and all the drawers and boxes and closets I could sneak my way into. While my parents visited with Grandma in the den, I found less boring things to occupy my attention. I found a treasure trove of knickknacks and doodads, ranging from old pocketknives to tobacco pipes to antique, dusty books. Then one Sunday I found a box of old black-and-white pictures in a closet. I tore into that box without a moment of hesitation, hot on the trail of an adventure that would allow me to imagine what it would've been like to live during the time I'd heard so much about from older relatives, including my own dad.

I spread the photos out on the bed. All the men in those pictures were wearing white shirts and thin black ties. On their heads were classy old hats, the kind Indiana Jones wore in *Raiders of the Lost Ark*. Nearly all of them had a cigarette dangling from their lips. None of them were smiling. The pictures were taken at various places, such as picnics, family reunions, wedding receptions, possibly even a holiday cookout. I noticed that the men were always congregated together, while the women were always standing in their own segregated group.

As I perused photo after photo, I became lost in my own little historical fantasy world. While I daydreamed, mesmerized by the untold stories of each of these mystical figures on old glossy paper, the door opened and my aunt Gwen walked in. She was my dad's sister and like a second mom to me.

"What do you have there, Clayton?" she asked with her trademark grin. She was a no-nonsense kind of woman, but she knew I was prone to mischief. We always had a special bond.

"Oh, nothing really; I just found some old pictures in here," I said, trying to play off the surprise of being caught in the act of digging through things that didn't belong to me.

"So you just found those pictures? Were they laying out on the bed or sitting on the desk? Or did you have to dig through the bottom of the closet to find them?" Before she even finished her questioning, she was sorting through the pictures that covered the bed with the zest of a woman who had discovered her own box of buried treasure. She knew almost every person in every photo and recalled details about them and their kids, their jobs, the farms they worked, and the people they married. Then she came to a picture that stopped her dead in her tracks. The color left her face. She stared at it for a moment, then said, "That's my daddy. He was your grandpa. He died the year before you were born." Even as a boy, I knew enough to realize the pain she felt when she picked up that photo of him.

Of course I wanted to know what happened to him, but regardless of the fact that she and I were buddies, she told me a bare minimum. The man that had been shrouded in secrecy was destined to remain there. I gathered only three basic facts from her about her father, my grandpa: he left them when she was a teenager, they saw him only occasionally after that, and he died before I was born.

She stacked all the photos neatly back in the box, placed the cover back on top, and slid it to the back of the closet where I'd found it. Then, as if to keep the lid on Pandora's box from ever opening again, she stacked a pair of old work boots on top of the cardboard sarcophagus that contained the remains of a corpse she never wanted to see again. It looked like she was experiencing physical pain as she closed the door to the closet and took my hand to lead me back into the den to join the family. Her reaction to the picture of my dad's father sank deep down into my bones. I intuitively knew that I could never ask my dad about him.

What If He Leaves?

I'd once overheard my mom talking to a friend about my father's emotional problems and how she thought they were the result of his dad walking out on him when he was young. When I was about four years old, my dad had a nervous breakdown. I remember some of his employees bringing him home from work, my mom opening up the screen door on the back porch, and my dad being unable to walk up the steps into the house because of his uncontrollable crying. I thought my dad was dying. I had recurring dreams for years in which that scene played over and over, but no one would ever talk to me about it. It wasn't until I was in college that my mom told me he had been hospitalized after that day and nearly lost his mind.

Even at a young age, I think I instinctively discerned that if I were to ask my dad about his dad, I would be dredging up hurtful things from the bottom of his heart that were best left alone. So I never asked. But in spite of how incredibly loving and faithful my own father was to me, my mom, and my brother, I carried a secret fear deep in my heart. *What will I do if Daddy leaves us one day like his daddy left him? How will I survive? Who will take care of us?* I lived with the heavy weight of that possibility for years. Sometimes I would even lie in bed and ask God, "Please, if my daddy is planning to leave us, don't let him go."

My father never gave me a single reason to doubt his commitment to us. He was a family man, first and foremost. But that didn't matter. Just the knowledge that his dad was able

---

The deep, visceral fear that stalked me day and night was that my dad would stop loving us. Once he stopped loving us, he would leave us.

---

to walk away made me wonder if, and when, my dad would leave us. And that was the singular force in my life that had the power to take my breath away in a split second. I tried to keep that thought out of my brain, because when it would slip up on me my breathing would get shallow and my skin would get sweaty and my ears would start ringing. My dad was my life. If he left, my life would end.

He arrived home from work every afternoon at 5:15 p.m. on the dot. Mom would have supper on the table. He would walk in the back door and I would be waiting for him. When I was little I would run as fast as I could and jump into his arms. He would pick me up and cradle me up near his face, kissing my cheek and my hair. I still remember the scruff of his beard tickling my nose and how his clothes smelled like varnish and paint from the shop where he worked. As I got older, I had to stop jumping on him because I was so big I nearly knocked him over.

If for some reason his black truck wasn't pulling into the driveway at 5:15, I went into emotional meltdown. I imagined that he had been killed in a car wreck or murdered at a gas station. As crazy as it sounds, those scenarios were preferable to the one I naturally assumed: that he had left our family and would never, ever come home again. At least if he'd died in an accident the departure wasn't of his own choosing. The deep, visceral fear that stalked me day and night was that my dad would stop loving us. Once he stopped loving us, he would leave us. Then I would be all alone without the man who had adopted me and given me a name and an identity and a family to belong to. I hoped he wasn't like his dad.

Learning to Live Defenseless but Unafraid

I didn't know what to call it back then. I was just a little boy. But now I understand that what I was wrestling with was a sense of *vulnerability*. I felt defenseless against the possibility that Daddy would abandon us. I knew that if he did, my mom and my brother and I would be vulnerable to the same sadness and loneliness that had affected my own father to the point of a nervous breakdown. I felt vulnerable on the inside, but I never said anything. I didn't know how to tell anyone how I felt. I didn't even possess the vocabulary to talk about it. And the one person I could absolutely never admit my fear to was my dad. It would've crushed him to know that I even ever thought he could leave me. I was ashamed to admit to him that I doubted him. Yet he was my best friend and the most trustworthy person in my life!

What would have changed in my heart and mind if I had made myself vulnerable to my dad, telling him how scared and defenseless I actually felt? But I didn't. That's the big mistake we so often make. Our innate sense of vulnerability paralyzes us in that place of fear. The one thing that will rescue us from this paralysis is trusting someone enough to open up to them about our sense of weakness, thus making ourselves vulnerable to them. It's as if we disarm the fear by turning it against itself, doing the thing that we're least likely to do—becoming vulnerable with someone by admitting how vulnerable we actually are.

///////

I had no idea how that worked as a little boy. My gut tells me that many of us still may not know how this works. It took me years to embrace even the idea that by confessing my weaknesses to God and others I would actually walk away stronger. But it's true. It's nuts, but it's true nonetheless.

James, the brother of Jesus, believed it was true. He encouraged his friends to practice vulnerability two thousand years ago when he wrote these words to them: "Confess your sins to each other and pray for each other so that you may be healed. The prayer of a righteous person is powerful and effective" (James 5:16). This Scripture reveals something surprising: the hard work of opening up to others and showing them your weaknesses and failures evidently has a healing element to it. In and of itself, the act of becoming vulnerable is cathartic, liberating, and healthy. It's also effective. Simply put, it actually works. Hiding our fears, shame, and shortcomings does nothing but shove us deeper into doubt and discouragement. We further isolate ourselves from the healing power of human connection and empathy.

One of my favorite writers of all time is G. K. Chesterton. He was British, Catholic, and a writer, thinker, and Christian apologist who never shied away from a good fight. He also had a knack for keen insight into matters that baffled other, lesser minds. My favorite Chesterton quote goes like this: "We men and women are all in the same boat, upon a stormy sea. We owe each other a terrible and tragic loyalty."[1] Indeed! We all go through the same storms, and we all need each other to survive. The human condition is weakness. It is difficulty and struggle and failure. None of us is immune and we're all "in the same boat," as it were. If we can remember this simple fact, that the people we need to be vulnerable with are just as vulnerable as we are, just as weak and insecure, then it's a little easier to open up with them without pretense or fear.

We also separate ourselves from God when we refuse to become vulnerable to the very One who knows us best and loves us most. John, one of Jesus's closest friends as well as one of his twelve handpicked disciples, wrote about the power of confession and vulnerability. Your relationship with God becomes stronger when you push past the shame and offer your true self to God without reservation. John writes, "If we confess our sins, he is faithful and just and will forgive us our sins and purify us from all unrighteousness" (1 John 1:9).

And this is exactly what Paul did over and over again in the letters he wrote to his friends scattered all over the ancient Mediterranean world. He didn't try to act tough. He refused to hide behind a façade of accomplishments. He readily and publicly confessed his sins. He boasted about his weaknesses. He showcased his hardships. He was vulnerable.

The Power of Vulnerability

Brene Brown has become known for her research on human connection. A quick search on YouTube will bring up clips of her talks, and you will immediately see how her insight has struck a nerve with people. Her videos have been viewed by tens of millions of people. I watched, intrigued, as she shared what she has learned over the years about how we are wired to connect with each other. She set out to find what makes humans truly happy. After twelve years of research, reading, surveys, and interviews, all the data led her to vulnerability. She defined *vulnerability* as emotional risk, exposure, and uncertainty toward being honest and seen.[2] To push through this uncertainty and risk requires courage. Becoming vulnerable is difficult because it carries with it the real possibility of being rejected, and thus feeling unloved. When we feel rejected and unloved, shame settles in as we question what it is about us that would make someone refuse to connect with us emotionally.

Brown has also discovered that human connection gives us a sense of purpose and meaning to life. This echoes what

God said at the very beginning of time, all the way back in the original garden where plant life, animal life, and human life all sprung into being at the command of the Creator: "It is not good for the man to be alone" (Gen. 2:18). Truly, we are wired to know and be known, to love and be loved, to see and be seen. God never intended for a single, solitary human to live life alone. Whether through marriage, friendship, or children, in order to thrive we innately need other people. Like Adam needed Eve, we are incomplete as disconnected individuals. In order to connect with others, we must be vulnerable. Brown writes:

> Owning our story can be hard but not nearly as difficult as spending our lives running from it. Embracing our vulnerabilities is risky but not nearly as dangerous as giving up on love and belonging and joy—the experiences that make us the most vulnerable. Only when we are brave enough to explore the darkness will we discover the infinite power of our light.[3]

Additionally, Brown discovered that shame is the fear of disconnection. In other words, we take it personally when we sense that someone is refusing to accept and love us as we

Deep down, we suspect that if God or the people around us saw us for who we really are, they would walk away.

really are. We internalize that sense of rejection as shame. This is precisely what happened in Eden when Adam and Eve sinned against God by disobeying his command to refrain from eating fruit from a certain tree that God had declared off-limits. Genesis 3:7 describes how they became aware of their nakedness and felt shame, and attempted to cover themselves so that they would not be truly seen by God. Ironically, God loved them completely and perfectly, but their failure to follow his command resulted in fear of rejection that manifested itself as shame—of failing, of being naked, of being rejected.

It is always fear that threatens to keep us from being vulnerable. That's why what people often project as strength—seeming to have it all together, to be unshakable and detached—is often not strength at all. When we act as if we are unable to be hurt, unaffected by the things that bring others pain, we are acting out of fear. We fear being exposed in any way that might subject us to more pain, humiliation, or rejection. Deep down, we suspect that if God or the people around us saw us for who we really are, they would walk away.

The remarkable message of the gospel is that God has in fact seen us at our worst, our most naked and exposed . . . and he didn't walk away. He moved toward us. A story from John's Gospel illustrates this perfectly. It's the longest recorded conversation between Jesus and any other person in the Bible. Jesus, a devout Jew, sat by a well and talked to a Samaritan woman—a woman who, by ethnicity and religion, would be considered unclean to an orthodox Jew. Let alone the fact that it would be uncouth for a prophet to be seen talking one-on-one to a woman at all. And all the more so when her story comes more into focus.

> A Samaritan woman came to draw water, and Jesus said to her, "Give me a drink." (His disciples had gone to the city to buy food.) The Samaritan woman said to him, "How is

it that you, a Jew, ask a drink of me, a woman of Samaria?"
(Jews do not share things in common with Samaritans.) Jesus
answered her, "If you knew the gift of God, and who it is
that is saying to you, 'Give me a drink,' you would have asked
him, and he would have given you living water." The woman
said to him, "Sir, you have no bucket, and the well is deep.
Where do you get that living water? Are you greater than
our ancestor Jacob, who gave us the well, and with his sons
and his flocks drank from it?" Jesus said to her, "Everyone
who drinks of this water will be thirsty again, but those who
drink of the water that I will give them will never be thirsty.
The water that I will give will become in them a spring of
water gushing up to eternal life." The woman said to him,
"Sir, give me this water, so that I may never be thirsty or have
to keep coming here to draw water."

Jesus said to her, "Go, call your husband, and come back."
The woman answered him, "I have no husband." Jesus said
to her, "You are right in saying, 'I have no husband'; for you
have had five husbands, and the one you have now is not your
husband. What you have said is true!" (John 4:7–18 NRSV)

We don't know why this woman had five husbands. What
we do know is that women in antiquity were not allowed
to divorce their husbands, and for a woman to be divorced
by her husband was to literally be cast aside, to be thrown
away. She was unable to work unless she became a prostitute.
So divorced women were often left at the mercy of distant
relatives to care for them. This woman had a number of
husbands, whatever the circumstances. Perhaps one or more
had died, perhaps one or more had walked away from her.
Either way, it's a story shrouded in pain and shame. In ancient
cultures, the stigma attached to being a divorced woman was

enormous. That's why she was at the well by herself drawing water at noon, the hottest time of the day. She was excluded from the daily ritual all the women kept of going to draw water together at daybreak in the cool of the morning.

Not only does this woman accept Jesus's offer with joy but she also goes and tells everyone in the town what had happened to her. And her testimony is very simple: "Come, see a man who told me everything I ever did" (v. 29). What a beautiful description of what it is to be seen by God. She met a Man who knew all the parts of her life and story that were painful and difficult, but he never flinched or looked away. She met a Man who accepted her in all the ways she was broken, without qualification or condition. She met a Man who saw her completely and without judgment, who was willing to speak boldly and truthfully with her. That is the story of the gospel. And that is the reason we can choose vulnerability rather than concealing our true selves out of fear—because we serve a God who already knows all the ways and places in which we are broken and damaged, and yet loves us and accepts us in those places without reservation and without hesitation.

The Moment of Truth

As a little boy, my greatest fear was losing the connection that I had with my father. If his dad could leave him, then he could leave me. And if he left me, it would have been my fault for not being a good enough son. But I lacked the courage to tell him how I felt. It seemed easier to live with the anxiety when he was ten minutes late for dinner than to risk exposing my fear of rejection to him. Looking back, I'm aware of the pain I inflicted on myself by bottling up all of that fear instead of releasing it by exposing it. My daddy had never taken advantage of my weakness or vulnerability as a boy. I knew he could be trusted. He had proven it countless times. Yet I was overcome with a sense of shame for even thinking that he may abandon me. I could never drag that fear out into the light. But one day, in an unexpected moment of raw honesty, my father became truly transparent with me about the most painful experience of his life. And my life was changed as a result of one vulnerable conversation.

///////

I was a senior in high school. It was my last semester before graduation. This particular spring day was hot and humid. I spent the morning outside with my dad, working in the yard like we had done together since I was a kid. My memories of him often include rakes, mulch, lawn mowers, and hedge trimmers. That day, he pointed out a dark cloud in the distance and predicted a thunderstorm in the next half hour. We put all our tools in the garage and headed inside before the rain came. Like clockwork, exactly thirty minutes later, the thunder and lightning began. Dad had grown up on a farm so he knew how to read the skies, but he was also deathly afraid of storms. A distant relative of his had been struck by lightning when he was young, and a friend's house had burned to the ground after a lightning strike in the early 1970s, so the protocol in our house at the first sign of a storm was to unplug everything electrical and, as an added precaution, flip the switches in the breaker box. We would all sit in silence and wait for the storm to pass, often in the dark.

The rest of the family was in another room, and my dad and I were in the den. As the storm rolled in, he began telling me about his childhood in rural South Carolina while loud thunder growled outside. To this day, I don't know why he decided to finally open up to me about his dad, but sitting there on the floor with him, I finally got to hear the truth about my mysterious grandfather. This was the first time I'd ever seen my dad really become vulnerable. He was digging deep and pulling up the most painful experience of his life, dragging it out into the open for me to look at.

Even as a strong young man, I recall being terrified at the thought of my dad finally breaking the silence about his father's abandonment. What would he tell me? Would he have another nervous breakdown by opening up this old wound? Sure, we had talked about personal things before, and he'd always been open about sharing experiences and memories of his childhood, but never once had he broached the topic of his dad. Until that moment.

He was ten years old, and every day after school he would rush home and finish his chores so that he could sit by the window. This was the best place to watch his dad pull into the driveway. When his dad would open the door to get out of his car, my daddy would run outside and hug Francis King around the leg or the waist. Then they would walk in the house together and sit down at the supper table with his mom, brother, and sister. The family would always eat together. But one day, he told me, his dad never came home. He waited there at the window until well after dark. His mom tried to get him to come eat supper, but he refused because it wouldn't be right to eat without his dad there. He went to bed hungry, forced to leave the chair by the window. He said,

"Something inside of me understood that my mama knew why Daddy didn't come home, but she wouldn't tell me. I wanted to know so bad but I didn't want to know, because I wanted to keep believing that he was coming home."

The next afternoon he sat by the window again as his mom busied herself with preparing the evening meal. He noticed that there were only four plates on the table when there had

I wanted to know so bad but I didn't want to know, because I wanted to keep believing that he was coming home.

always been five. "When I asked Mama where the other plate was, she told me that Daddy didn't need a plate because he wasn't going to be there for supper that night," he said. "Then she said he would never be there for supper again. Ever. She said he was gone and he wasn't coming back."

The words tore through my heart like a wildfire. My dad started to cry. He didn't even try to stop the tears. I guess the years of holding back the pain had worn down his resolve. He dumped it out all at once as the rain came down in sheets and the thunder rumbled. He said, "I sat there at the window every day for three weeks waiting on Daddy to come home from work. I didn't want to believe that Mama was telling the truth. And every day at the window, I felt the shame of not having a daddy getting stronger. It was a small farming community and everybody knew he was gone. Back in those days, it was an embarrassment for children not to have a daddy. I wondered every day what I did to make him leave us. I blamed myself. I thought I was a stupid kid. That my grades weren't good. I always had sloppy handwriting, so I even wondered if that was why he left us. I just assumed it was my fault. I wasn't good enough as a son to make him want to stay."

I was at a loss for words. All I could do was cry with him. The revelation of not only what happened but also how it had made my dad feel for forty years was a hard blow. I finally managed to ask him one question, the one that I had wondered about since that day in my grandmother's house when I discovered the box of old pictures.

"Why? Why did he leave?"

The look of despair on his face was a mixture of sadness and resignation. He stared off into a distant place, eyes glazed over and listless. "He left us for another woman. He had a girlfriend on the side. He loved her. He told Mama that he was going to leave and live with her. She didn't have the courage to tell us until I finally had the courage to ask her. One day I was sitting at the window waiting on him when she came in and told me he was never coming home, and I might as well forget about seeing him again. I got upset and started crying, and I said, 'What makes you so sure he's not coming home? Maybe he just had to take a trip somewhere. How do you know?' Then she told me the truth, and nothing has ever hurt me like what she said." He waved his hands in the air just like my grandma did when she talked. In his mind's eye he was reliving that moment as if it had happened yesterday.

"'Your daddy left us for another woman. He told me that he's going to marry her and live with her from now on. So stop moping around and pouting, get away from that window, and help me clean up this kitchen. He's not coming home.'

Just like that." Those were the words that would change his life forever. Then, silence. Neither one of us spoke. It seemed like a week passed by as we sat in the thickness of what he had just shared. I was afraid to move, afraid to talk, afraid to breathe. It was a holy moment, fierce and unforgiving. My father had peeled back the scar tissue, slicing through the tough exterior he'd been hiding behind for four decades, and he had invited me inside to see the carnage that was still as fresh as the day the emotional earthquake had laid his insides to waste. I was humbled at the invitation to come inside. But once I got there, I was painfully aware of how big and horrible that pain had grown over the years. I knew that we had gone over the edge of a cliff and there would be no turning back, no way to recover, no returning to a place of secrets and privacy. The great big scary cat was out of the bag.

Vulnerability Is an Invitation to Intimacy

My father had shown me the deepest part of himself, as a man and a son. I immediately and irreversibly loved my dad more than I had just an hour earlier. How it happened I do not know, but all of a sudden there was extra grace in my heart for my father. Though he was a good man, he was flawed and far from perfect. He was impatient, prone to fits of rage, and often distant and preoccupied. He was hard on me and my brother at times and was known by his employees to be a fair and honest man but difficult to work for. His temper could flare in an instant, and more than once I watched him kick, throw, stomp, and break things in the garage or his shop when he was frustrated.

158

That day, in a flash, it all made sense! The reason he was prone to fits of frustration, his unannounced angry outbursts, the occasions when he would lose control and yell at one of us . . . it was all because of his dad. He felt rejected. Unloved. Ashamed and embarrassed. Abandoned. And he blamed himself. He thought it was his fault. Blame is a way to expel the anger and frustration we feel. That's what he'd been doing for forty years. But in the span of half an hour, he had chosen to crack open that vault where his most hideous pain had remained hidden. He walked me through the door and down the stairs to the very bottom, below the subfloor, below the cellar, to the bedrock of his identity as a man. I felt like someone had taken me into a secret chamber of the White House, or the Great Pyramids, or the Temple Mount, and I was gazing on treasures whose value surpassed estimation. The currency we shared that afternoon was vulnerability, and I had just hit the jackpot.

I placed my hand on his shoulder and spoke softly. I remember those words well, because I believe it was the first time my father and I spoke to one another as men. "Daddy, I am so

---

The currency we shared that afternoon was vulnerability, and I had just hit the jackpot.

---

sorry that he left you. But it wasn't your fault. You didn't do anything to deserve that. I wish you'd had a dad half as good as you, because you've been the best father a boy could ever have. I love you so much, and I am glad you didn't leave us."

Gasping for words between tearful breaths, he replied to me earnestly, "I decided when we adopted you that I wouldn't ever put you through what my daddy made me live with. It hurts right now just as much as the day he disappeared. I'd give anything if I could've had him come to my ball games or show me how to fix a leaky faucet. It's too late now. He's dead and gone, and I've tried to put it behind me my whole life. Funny thing is, it's still right here with me. It didn't go anywhere. I should've told you about all this before now, but you were too young and I didn't want to hurt you. I wanted to wait until you were a man and you could handle it. I guess today was the day."

From that day forward, my father and I were never the same. We were stronger. We related to one another in a new way. There was an understanding we didn't have before. His demeanor toward me even changed. I was still his son, but I also became his friend. When we talked, there was a greater sense of trust and a stronger sense of intimacy. It would be that way until his death. The closeness we shared after that afternoon thunderstorm was a true gift of God. Little did I know that when he became vulnerable with me that Saturday, it would be the beginning of a long season in which vulnerability would become an everyday reality. He would eventually need me to do everything for him in a way that made keeping any kind of secret impossible.

The day before he died, I sat by his bed and rubbed his arms and feet. We talked off and on all day long as he slipped in and out of consciousness. He knew that death was imminent, so he made sure to give me some final instructions regarding his personal effects. He told me over and over that he loved me and my brother and our children. Yet the one thing that stands out to me was what he said about his father just hours before he died.

"Son, would you believe that right now I am thinking about my daddy? I miss him so much. I don't know why I want to see him so bad, right before I die, but I guess some hurts never go away. I'm taking what he did to me all the way to the grave. But I forgive him for it. God used those hard times to teach me a lot and to make me a better man. But mostly, I realized that I did have a daddy. God became my father and he was always there, and he never left me. He's still with me right now, all the way to the end."

The next day my dad died. I preached my father's funeral on Father's Day. My earthly father met his heavenly Father face-to-face on Father's Day. How appropriate. No more shame. No more blame. No more pain or rejection. As I lost my father, he was finally with his.

Come to think of it, I didn't lose my dad. I know exactly where he is.

/// **8**

UNDERSTANDING

You Don't Have to Waste
Your Weakness

Any fool can know. The point is to understand.

Albert Einstein[1]

Love allows understanding to dawn, and understanding is precious. Where you are understood, you are at home. Understanding nourishes belonging. When you really feel understood, you feel free to release yourself into the trust and shelter of the other person's soul.

John O'Donohue, *Anam Cara:*
A Book of Celtic Wisdom

When it really hit me that both my parents had died before I turned forty, I wondered how I would go on living without them. All I wanted was to understand what had happened. I avoided people with trite answers and quick explanations. I was magnetically drawn to people who understood what I had gone through, primarily people who had known similar losses. They got me. They could help me. They had something I could hang on to. Jerry Sittser was one such person.

Dr. Sittser, a professor at Whitworth University, was already writing about discerning the will of God before a nightmarish accident changed his life forever: a single car crash took the lives of his wife, mother, and young daughter. In one terrible moment, three generations of his family were lost. Sittser doesn't gloss over the trauma of his experience, but he shares the understanding he's gained through his own suffering with the rest of us. As his story has been told in books and sermons that have gone around the world, speaking honestly about his weakness and loss but also to the veracity of Christian hope, thousands of hurting people have gained understanding in their own trauma—because of the faithful witness of this one man who continues to proclaim the hope of resurrection in the face of such great sorrow. His books, including *The Will of God as a Way of Life* and *A Grace Disguised*, have been a source of understanding for many.

In the words of Sittser himself:

Gifts of grace come to all of us. But we must be ready to see and willing to receive these gifts. It will require a kind of sacrifice, the sacrifice of believing that, however painful our losses, life can still be good—good in a different way than before, but nevertheless good. I will never recover from my loss and I will never get over missing the ones I lost. But I still cherish life. . . . I will always want the ones I lost back again. I long for them with all my soul. But I still celebrate the life I have found because they are gone. I have lost, but I have also gained. I lost the world I loved, but I gained a deeper awareness of grace. That grace has enabled me to clarify my purpose in life and rediscover the wonder of the present moment.[2]

That is the kind of understanding that comes to us through hard times—the awareness of grace that brings a clarity of purpose into our present moment. Pain awakens us to the reality of God's hope in ways that we could not have understood before it. As C. S. Lewis famously said, pain grabs us, holds our attention, and, when yielded to God, offers us understanding. Pain can have a purpose. "But pain insists upon being attended to. God whispers to us in our pleasures, speaks in our conscience, but shouts in our pains: It is His megaphone to rouse a deaf world."[3]

Before my own losses, I had preached the gospel, proclaiming the hope of resurrection all over the world. And I did believe it—as best as I could before I tasted true weakness. But when I preached the funeral of each of my parents (and seven other relatives in a short period of time), I realized that in the moments after their deaths I understood the reality of resurrection hope in ways I simply could not have before. What I'd believed in my head now became true in my heart—an understanding of just how tangible, how concrete our hope in Christ really is.

Understanding Is Greater than Information

In Western culture, and all the more in this digital age, our idea of learning is almost exclusively about consuming information. Our access to knowledge and facts is unlimited and unparalleled. We consume countless images, ideas, and opinions, more than we could possibly ever know what to do with. The sheer amount of information that's constantly at our fingertips has a paralyzing effect on our minds. The truth is, when it comes to real life in general and life with God in particular, we simply cannot become the kinds of people we ought to be through head knowledge alone. Our experiences transform us—and that transformation has more to do with what happens in our hearts than in our heads.

//////

What God wants to do in and through the difficult seasons of our lives is not to give us *information* but to give us *understanding*. God may never give you an intellectual understanding of your suffering. In fact, I find that to rarely be the case. Seldom will you find easily discernible "reasons" for the depth or timing of your hardship. We live in a world where the kingdom of God has not yet been fully realized on the earth, and in the meantime there are many things we can and must experience that we cannot make sense of with our intellect.

Of course there are always people who will attempt to give easy answers to why you go through hard times and cite chapter and verse to do it. Some people want to assign blame. Some presume to know all the purposes of God in our pain. (Speaking of suffering, those are the most insufferable kinds of people to talk to when times are truly hard.) When we try to understand suffering exclusively in our heads, our tendency is to isolate our hearts from the process, and the heart matters more than we might imagine. Hard times can't be sterilized, placed under a microscope, or dissected. Just as it's futile to attempt to describe the breathtaking nature of your first view from the rim of the Grand Canyon, it's also an exercise in futility to try to make intellectual sense of your weakness until you've experienced the full brunt of that weakness with your emotions. *You have to feel it before you can understand it.*

God does want to give us *understanding,* in the best and deepest sense of the word. But it's not the kind of understanding that empowers us to play God and explain everything that's happening. That kind of "understanding," no matter how wrapped up it is in religious language, is always shallow and superficial. The understanding God wants to give us is an experiential understanding of being truly human that makes us more available to others and less smug and self-righteous.

This broken world doesn't need more "experts." What's more helpful are broken people who are allowing God to heal them and make them stronger as a result of their weakness. Those kinds of people (like me and like you) can and will

---

Weakness is the doorway to understanding, and understanding is the doorway to compassion and ministry.

---

be used by God for the sake of helping others. As much as we don't want to hear it, weakness is the doorway to understanding, and understanding is the doorway to compassion and ministry.

When we understand a person's situation and emotions, when we can say, "I've been there too," we are able to join them on their journey through hard times and help them.

Unless we understand something of what they're facing and what they're feeling, our attempts to help can come across as little more than well-meaning advice.

When we've tasted some of the same bitterness they're experiencing, when we've absorbed a kind of pain that's similar to what they're going through, we stand equipped to enter into their hardship in a way that gives us credibility. We've walked that road. We can say with true integrity, "I know how you feel." This is understanding, and there's no other way to get it but to plumb the depths of pain and weakness ourselves . . . and to survive by walking out the other side stronger than when we walked into it.

It is not abstract understanding. It is the kind of understanding that comes, in Henri Nouwen's words, from "drinking the cup all the way to the bottom" for ourselves.[4] It is a very different thing to suffer loss in a way that cuts us deeply, as opposed to observing pain from afar as disconnected bystanders. C. S. Lewis writes about this eloquently in *A Grief Observed*, after losing his wife, Joy, the love of his life, after only a few short years of marriage:

> We were even promised sufferings. They were part of the programme. We were even told, "Blessed are they that mourn" and I accepted it. I've got nothing that I hadn't bargained for. Of course it is different when the thing happens to oneself, not to others, and in reality, not in imagination.[5]

The Most Dangerous Prayer You Can Pray

Be careful what you pray for, because God may decide to give it to you after all. That's what happened to me. I began my

Christian journey as an adolescent who wanted to change the world for Jesus. The first prayer I remember praying after my conversion to faith in Christ was simply, "Jesus, use me." Have you ever thought of how crazy that sounds? You'd never say that on a first date. You wouldn't say that to your boss after a week on the job. You wouldn't even say that to your parents or your spouse! How absurd to ever say to anyone, "Just use me." But we do ask Jesus to use us, because he is altogether good, trustworthy, and wise. This simple prayer is undergirded by an understanding that Jesus would use us only in good ways that grow us and glorify him, so we don't hesitate to ask him to do something we wouldn't ever ask another to do.

I couldn't possibly have predicted how God would answer that prayer or the kaleidoscope of struggles and hardships he would employ to actually prepare me to be used for his purposes in the lives of others. Because of the hell I've gone through, I understand how other people feel when they're going through hell. I keep my mouth shut and listen when they scream, curse, and rant about how unfair life is. I understand how they feel. We tend to pray, "Jesus, use me," with the unconscious assumption that he will do it in some grand, epic way that will make us feel important and indispensable to God's ultimate plan. And to be sure, we are valuable to God and his ultimate plan of redeeming all of creation. However, our visions of exactly how God will use us may not always be accurate. Put plainly, it may hurt a little more than we had anticipated and it may take a little longer than we had planned for.

When we ask God to use us, we're giving him a green light to lead us into, and through, some really hard things.

But without those experiences, we would never know the difficulties other people have seen and we wouldn't know how to reach out to them, listen to them, and lean into their weakness. Understanding comes from experiencing—experiencing weakness and adversity for ourselves. There's just no shortcut. The reason why people need ministry is because they are hurting, wounded, and messed up. In order for us to grow

> *Understanding comes from experiencing—experiencing weakness and adversity for ourselves. There's just no shortcut.*

and change, to become healthy and whole, Jesus uses us to help each other through the scariest seasons of life. So the hard times we've endured and the scars we've received aren't random at all. God has been leveraging them for his own purpose: to train and teach and prepare us to "be used" in the lives of others in order to help them through their hard times, hard times we have already gone through. Our seasons of weakness are not just for *our transformation*. They are also for *our preparation* in becoming a tool for good in God's hands, to help others.

Personally, I'm not prepared to help someone who's been sexually abused, beyond praying with them and pointing them to a more qualified person for care. But my wife, Sharie, has an immediate understanding because she experienced sexual abuse at the hands of a stepfather for nearly five years. God did not orchestrate the abuse, but my wife leverages that awful experience for the sake of helping others. You don't have to have an airtight explanation ready. You don't need all the answers to every conceivable question someone may ask you. You just need to tell your story of how you made it. Be willing to talk about your grief and confusion and anger. Open up. Let them know that you understand.

I know that, for me, losing my parents eighteen months apart was unspeakably painful. I reached out for help to a litany of people: a Christian counselor, several pastors, a few good friends, my wife. But I found the greatest comfort in being able to talk to a few other guys who had lost their fathers around the same time that my dad died. All four of them were pastors, and each of them was close to my age, so we were all in a similar season of life. Two of them were close friends and two of them were acquaintances whom I respected. Jud Wilhite, Perry Noble, Judah Smith, and Steven Furtick knew the same grief I wrestled with because they lost their fathers around the same time I lost mine. And in a strange twist, the same friend who had comforted me when my mother died with his own story of losing his mom actually lost his dad just a few months before I lost mine. Perry was there for me, again. It didn't comfort me that their fathers were dead, but it comforted me to know that I wasn't the only one going through this pain. *If they could survive, so could I.*

I knew that they understood. Sometimes that's all it takes to get through the hard times. These men had authority to speak to my situation because they knew the road I was traveling. Not only could they say "I understand" with honesty and integrity but they also had a level of understanding I needed to draw from. This is the hard part. The only way we reach that level of understanding is through experience. If I ask God to increase my patience, it may mean getting stuck in a traffic jam on the way to the airport or learning to parent a toddler. If my self-control level is at five and I want it to be at nine, the only way to push through that barrier is to be stretched beyond anything I've ever known. The harder we fight to understand a truth, the longer we will remember it. It sticks with us because we fight hard to get it.

A friend who's an ultramarathoner put it in concise terms for me one day: "I know that I can ride a bike for a hundred miles because I actually did it. Until that day, I never got past eighty miles. I was stuck there for years and thought that was my limit. Now when I want to quit and my legs and lungs are screaming at me to stop, I have a deeper understanding of what I am capable of because I've already done it. I have muscle memory that tells me I can do more than I feel like I can do. The pain of that extra twenty miles proved to me that I could go farther. It gave me a better understanding of how strong I actually could be."

A Deep, Visceral Knowing

I'm fascinated by the way God made the brain. When something hurts us or is hard to go through, our brains begin working frantically to tell the rest of our bodies what to do, sending impulses and firing off synapses through millions of nerve endings, up and down our spines and to our vital organs. When our bodies detect pain or stress, they go into survival mode, releasing chemicals like cortisol, endorphins, and adrenaline that keep us alive; this response is commonly called "fight or flight," and it gives us the wherewithal to get out of harm's way, the speed to outrun a predator, or the wits we need to protect our loved ones from danger.

Because of the strength of these chemicals that make our heart rate skyrocket, our breathing become shallow, and our muscles tremble, the memories associated with fear, anxiety, stress, and pain are irreversibly locked into our brains. Pain has a way of sticking around even after it's long gone. Neurologists tell us that we never really forget traumatic moments and events. God designed us to remember them for the benefit of the understanding we gain as a result of experiencing them.

In a nutshell, *we don't fully know what we can endure until we are forced to endure more than we've ever endured.* We don't fully grasp how strong God really is until he allows us to walk through a season of total weakness in which we must fully rely on him in complete desperation. This is the source of understanding. It's a deep knowing of a thing, a visceral and tangible experience that changes us down to our bone marrow. Even after the pain has subsided, it still hasn't

---

There's nothing more powerful than being able to say to someone who's hurting, "I know how you feel. I've been there too."

---

fully left the premises because the memory remains, and as long as we have the memory we have a truer understanding of what it means to be fully human, fully flawed, and utterly in need of the grace of God and the presence of others to get us through the hard times. That understanding gives us the authority to tenderly enter into another person's weakness and stand with them. It proves that we're no rookies to this fallen world. We're not surprised or put off when things fall apart or the bottom falls out. We understand now. So take that understanding and help others with it. There's nothing more powerful than being able to say to someone who's hurting, "I know how you feel. I've been there too."

That's how God takes everything, even the bad things, and leverages them for something good. In the immortal words of the apostle Paul, "In all things God works for the good of those who love him, who have been called according to his purpose" (Rom. 8:28).

The Story of Lazarus

The source of our understanding doesn't come from us but from God, who has a profound understanding of us. Even for God, understanding is not an abstract, detached affair. In Jesus Christ, he has chosen to understand human weakness the same way we come to understand weakness in the lives of others—from fully entering into a weakness of his own. He became one of us. Jesus, like us, experienced deep human fulfillment through deep, abiding friendships. Like anyone else, he had people he uniquely poured into and who uniquely poured into him. One of those people was a man named Lazarus.

Lazarus was Jesus's friend. He was not a random spectator, not another face in the crowd just looking for a miracle. He was one of the people Jesus could live the beautiful ordinary of everyday life with. We all know Jesus loved everyone. But like anyone else would, he had a special kind of affection for the handful of people who were his truest and best friends, like Lazarus. While out traveling and teaching, Jesus got word that Lazarus was sick back in Bethany. As the greatest miracle worker the world has ever known, all Jesus had to do was speak the word, even from afar, and Lazarus would have been healed. But much to the dismay of Lazarus's sisters, Mary and Martha, with whom Jesus had also shared many meals, he did not come to see his friend immediately. In fact, after Martha sent word to Jesus that he needed to come heal her sick brother, he lingered for two more days before he returned to Bethany.

For Mary and Martha, the delay felt cold and calloused, as if Jesus didn't understand the seriousness of the situation. Yet ironically enough, understanding seemed to be precisely Jesus's purpose, but on a much broader scale. As he was doing the work of the ministry, he wanted the disciples to understand his mission. Jesus unapologetically wanted to embrace the kind of understanding he could gain only from suffering the loss of his friend in the ways that we all do. Moreover, he wanted Mary and Martha to understand that he could do more than just *heal the sick*—he could actually *raise the dead*.

Throughout the entire story, we see the relentless focus of Jesus to go straight through the valley of the shadow of death rather than using his powers to avoid it and walk around it. While on their ministry trip, the disciples didn't want Jesus to go through Judea, remembering how the residents had tried to stone Jesus the last time he went there. But Jesus insisted on going right back into the heart of darkness to face the potentially hostile crowds without shrinking away. He was not looking to skirt the hard times but to face them head-on without flinching. Jesus knew that we must lean into our pain, so he chose not to avoid the unfriendly crowds that awaited him in Judea. Nor did he avoid the grief of facing the death of a close friend. Just as steering your car into a skid instead of away is the only way to correct the vehicle when it starts to slide out of control, Christ takes a direct line to painful places that most of us would steer clear of if we could.

Like us, Mary and Martha lacked understanding. Like us, the intensity of their own pain was so great there was no way, in the moment, they could get a sense of what Jesus was really up to. That is the nature of losing someone or something we love—the sense of loss can be so profound it swallows up any other thought or emotion. The pain of the moment reverberates in our heads and in our stomachs, without relief.

By the time Jesus finally got to the scene, it was far too late. Lazarus was dead. And he died while Jesus delayed. Don't you feel like that sometimes? While you're waiting on Jesus to come through for you, to meet a need or answer a prayer, he just seems to be . . . waiting? While you feel like you're dying, he just keeps delaying. The friends and family of Lazarus felt that confusion and frutration. Jesus can do the miracle, can heal Lazarus, so *where is he*? Why hasn't he answered?

In antiquity, people believed that the spirit hovered around the corpse for the first three days. But by the time Jesus arrived in Bethany, Lazarus had been dead for four days. He was not just dead but very dead—corpse-rotting, stinking kind of dead. Lacking understanding of the unparalleled power at work in Jesus, Lazarus's sister Martha cried out in pain and accusation, "Lord . . . if you had been here, my brother would not have died" (John 11:21). As it was in the ancient Jewish psalms, their relationship with God (in Jesus) was not one of delicacy but of intimacy. They didn't attempt to rationalize or explain their own pain but rather they hurled their hurt directly at Jesus. Strangely enough,

God always seems partial to people who speak to him with such searing honesty.

Jesus was not indifferent to the pain of his friends, as we can see in the shortest but perhaps most poignant verse in the Bible: "Jesus wept" (v. 35). In the same way that Lazarus's sisters unleashed their grief without reserve, Jesus unleashed his own grief over their loss—wave after wave of grief. The weeping of Jesus was so profound that the crowds said, "See how he loved him" (v. 36). Jesus was fully human, and who can be fully human without experiencing the soul-splitting grief of losing someone you love?

Like any great teacher, Jesus didn't attempt to answer the questions with answers but rather with more questions of his own that would force his listeners to grasp the truth for themselves. So Jesus asked the grieving Martha, "Did I not tell you that if you believe, you will see the glory of

They already knew that Jesus could heal the sick. They didn't yet understand that he could raise the dead.

God?" (v. 40). By fully entering into the moment, Jesus first embraced a deep understanding of the people around him. But he had also come to give them a different kind of understanding. He wanted them to understand that the power of resurrection was right there, right then, and that there was no resurrection without the person who was himself stronger than death. They already knew that Jesus could heal the sick. They didn't yet understand that he could raise the dead.

Jesus always reveals himself to us in the moments of our greatest need. And while it may not make our suffering feel worthwhile at the time, one of the blessings of those times is that we come to see things about God that people generally just don't see. It's not that Jesus doesn't want to reveal himself to all of us but that he often reveals himself to those who need him most—*when* they need him most. And so Mary and Martha, though their grief was great, were also the first recipients of an earth-shattering revelation: "I am the resurrection and the life. The one who believes in me will live, even though they die" (v. 25).

Long before any of the rest of us came to understand anything about death and resurrection through the cross of Jesus, Mary and Martha beat us all to the punch. It surely took great restraint for Jesus not to heal Lazarus earlier, in order to bring quick relief to his sisters. But Jesus didn't come to bring *temporary relief*. He came to give us *everlasting hope*. He came to bring the revelation of resurrection. So Jesus did the unimaginable. Speaking with the same authority as the One who spoke creation into existence, the voice of Jesus, moments before contorted in grief, thundered out the words, "Lazarus, come out!" And after it was too late even for a miracle, Lazarus came walking out of the grave still wrapped in grave clothes. Mary and Martha didn't just listen to a lesson. They lived to see a resurrection.

Resurrection could not have been grasped with their minds—they had to have the mystery revealed to them experientially, firsthand. For two days after he had been told Lazarus was ill, and knowing the heartbreak of those he loved, Jesus kept relentless focus on the broader task he came to accomplish. Though the pain would be great, the understanding would be greater. He could never explain any of this to them—he could only lead them into an experience. They were never going to understand the mystery of resurrection through the lecture of a rabbi. They had to witness a mummy ascend from within a tomb.

///////

The raising of Lazarus was a hope and a shadow of the resurrection to come. It was the coming glory of the kingdom of God being revealed in a small burst, to be followed by Jesus's own resurrection and, ultimately, one day ours as well. With an understanding of resurrection and a hope that it will one day be ours, we can endure, we can abide—we can remain steadfast even in the doubt, as Mary and Martha did when they worshiped Jesus even though they could not understand how he could let their brother die.

In the moment, Mary and Martha had no understanding of resurrection at all—which is almost always true during adversity. There are moments when we can't see anything past our own pain. Yet in the end, not only did Lazarus's sisters receive a deeper understanding of God but millions of other people also have. Think about this for a moment: throughout the centuries, in thousands of cultures and languages, the understanding of God's greatest power has been told and retold through the resurrection story of Lazarus. What started out as unbearable grief ended with an understanding of the God of resurrection that has swept over countless lives. That is at least part of God's agenda in your own struggles: to give you an understanding that will not only bring comfort and perspective but also ultimately open you up to many others who will need to drink of the hope you have received.

Clarity of Purpose in Our Suffering

I do want to give a cautionary word here. There have been many well-intentioned people who have caused even deeper pain for people in their weakness by telling them, however delicately it might be worded, something like this: "God did all of this to teach you a lesson." I do not believe that God orchestrates all our tragedies just for the sake of teaching us something. What I do believe is that God uses our struggles to allow us to experience him in ways we never have before. Again, we rarely know the reasons why we struggle in particular ways and particular places in our lives, only that none of it will be wasted when God is in the mix. Suffering places us in a posture of humility that makes understanding possible. Adversity can bring great clarity as it forces us to look hard for a purpose, purifying our motives and clarifying our true beliefs and convictions about God and life.

As it was for Mary and Martha, I was not going to be sustained by an intellectual understanding of resurrection while in the depths of my own depression. I needed to experience the hope of resurrection life that cannot be felt until we have entered into desperation ourselves. While it is hard to explain, a tangible sense of the presence of God and a deep knowing of the reality of gospel hope are gifts we are not able to receive until our own pain has busted us wide open. The beautiful thing is that once we have received this truth through real experience, we become conduits of the grace of God that can flow through us to others.

Any true revelation of God, however much it might comfort and strengthen us, can never be meant for us alone. We experience God in the depths of confusion so that his power can flow through us in a way that enables us to understand the resurrection power that's been made known to us. It is only this kind of first-person experience that can impart to us the wisdom that cannot be taught—only revealed. Then we too are able to show the world small bursts of resurrection, a glimpse of kingdom come, a foretaste of the great resurrection we long for.

Now you can understand what God can do with your struggles. You can have some clarity in your adversity. He "comforts us in all our troubles," Paul writes, "so that we can comfort those in any trouble with the comfort we ourselves receive from God" (2 Cor. 1:4).

///**9**

WORSHIP

Finally Giving Up the Illusion
of Control

Every man becomes the image of the God
he adores.
He whose worship is directed to a dead
thing becomes dead.
He who loves corruption rots.
He who loves a shadow becomes, himself,
a shadow.
He who loves things that must perish lives
in dread of their perishing.

Thomas Merton,
No Man Is an Island

We do not want you to be uninformed, brothers
and sisters, about the troubles we experienced in

the province of Asia. We were under great pressure, far beyond our ability to endure, so that we despaired of life itself. Indeed, we felt we had received the sentence of death. But this happened that we might not rely on ourselves but on God, who raises the dead. He has delivered us from such a deadly peril, and he will deliver us again. On him we have set our hope that he will continue to deliver us, as you help us by your prayers. *Then many will give thanks on our behalf* for the gracious favor granted us in answer to the prayers of many.

2 Corinthians 1:8–11, emphasis added

I was driving my son to preschool one morning, my mind consumed with a thousand thoughts. The radio played in the background, but I had no idea what song it was or who was singing it. My four-year-old son was talking to me from the backseat, but the words weren't registering. I was preoccupied with many cares and concerns, and as the thoughts flooded my mind it raced in a dozen directions, and I found myself mentally paralyzed. This was a common, daily occurrence during that season of my life, as I tried to juggle all my responsibilities as a dad, husband, pastor, and president of a nonprofit . . . not to mention the ever-increasing stress of caring for my parents, whose physical and mental health were failing fast.

Suddenly my eyes caught something to my right. I snapped my head in that direction and noticed a church sign. It had been there every day for years. I passed it multiple times a day on my way to town or to take the boys to school. It never said anything significant, at least to me, so it had just become part of the landscape, a simple piece of the scenery. But on that day, there was a message for me on that church sign. I think God may have placed it there specifically for Clayton King. It read, "You are never stronger than when you are on your knees."

The paradox of that statement was like a cold bucket of water to my face. I felt like my life was out of control. I was consumed with worry. I was watching my parents become more addicted to prescription painkillers as they grew weaker and more frail. The only conversations I ever had with them revolved around their bodies and minds breaking down. Meanwhile my wife and I were raising two small children, I was traveling 150 days a year speaking in churches and conferences and colleges, I was leading a staff, and my wife and I were under a major deadline for our new book on marriage. I didn't feel strong in any area. I felt weak. I was weak! It took two strong cups of coffee just to get me going in the mornings. I was sleeping only a few hours a night, so I was tired and grumpy all day, and by two o'clock every day I was looking for a place to sit or lie down so that I could attempt to sneak a nap in between items on my ever-growing to-do list. And for the first time in my life, I was experiencing depression.

The thing about that church sign that grabbed hold of me was how simple the message was and how perfectly it related to how I felt. My strength was gone. I was running on fumes. The strong, healthy leader who had always been able to push through the hardest seasons was worn-out and empty. But I had enough good sense to know that God was my only hope, so it became a daily ritual for me to fall on my knees in my study, usually around 5:00 a.m. when I would wake up, and beg God for the strength to make it through that day. Not the week or the month, just enough for the day. I never *felt* strong down on my knees. I felt weak, which is why I was kneeling every morning. But something about that message on that sign I had passed for years spoke to me. *Was I really stronger when I was on my knees?*

Singing through the Pain

When I got the call that my dad had passed away, I was literally getting in the car to drive to hospice in hopes that I could be with him when he died. But I didn't make it. The pain of regret settled down hard on my shoulders. My wife offered to drive, and I took her up on it. I sat in the passenger seat and began to wallow in self-pity as we made the drive to the room where we had just left my dad a few hours earlier. How would I ever forgive myself for not being there with him when he died? How would I ever be able to wipe the image out of my mind of my dad dying all alone in that room with no one by his side?

When we arrived at the hospice home, I walked in with Sharie and our boys. We were holding hands. The sun was just cresting the eastern horizon and the June air was already warm and humid. I was going to have to walk into a room where my father's dead body was lying on a bed. Somehow I was going to have to face the fact that he was gone. I felt like I was trudging through wet cement as I came to the door that led into his room. I turned to face my family. "I would like to go in there by myself first," I said. "I need a few minutes with Daddy alone. I'll come get you guys when I'm ready for you to come in too."

My legs felt as weak as water. I could hardly stand up. But I pushed the door open and took two steps before I saw him. He was lying on his back. A bed sheet was covering him from the waist down. He was wearing his pajama shirt. His eyes were closed and his mouth was slightly open. His hair was clean and white, brushed back like he'd always worn it. And his hands were folded over his chest, holding a single yellow rose. Yellow was my mom's favorite color. She wore a yellow dress to my wedding. My dad picked out a yellow dress for her when she died. She was buried in that yellow dress.

And then it hit me. A feeling so foreign to me that I still struggle to describe it. A hot wave of grief engulfed me and my body broke out in a sweat. I began to shake; it emanated from my core. It took a few seconds, but I could feel the tears gathering until they finally poured out like water from

---

The weeping was involuntary, almost like vomiting, but the only thing that left my body was sadness and salty tears.

---

a couple of fire hydrants. The weeping was involuntary, almost like vomiting, but the only thing that left my body was sadness and salty tears.

Almost in a trance, I stepped over to the bed and placed my hand on my dad's cheek. It was cold and smooth. Then I touched his hair, brushing it back over his head, remembering all the times as a little boy that I would sit on his lap and do that very thing with his hair until I fell asleep.

I touched his hands and traced his fingers, remembering how my father had made a living and created a life for our family with those hands. He was a mechanic and a carpenter, a plumber and an electrician, and the same hands that had fixed countless problems were the hands that had comforted me and my mom and my brother when we needed love and care. Then . . . sobs. Wailing and weeping. The taste of salt running into the corners of my mouth. A growing pond of snot and tears at my feet. I felt like I was going to pass out. I leaned forward and placed both hands on the edge of the bed. I labored to catch my breath. I looked at Daddy again. His color wasn't right. He looked pale. Then I remembered he was dead. I was in excruciating agony.

Without thinking about what I was actually doing, I slowly raised both arms toward heaven. Standing beside my father's body, like a force had taken over my will, I involuntarily began to sing "Great Is Thy Faithfulness."

As I sang of God's unfailing, unchanging compassion and mercy, an awareness of how things really were slowly replaced my feeling of helplessness. My father was not in that dead body. He was with God. The more I sang, the brighter the room seemed to grow. The shame and regret I felt for not being by his side when he passed away subsided for a moment as I imagined Jesus standing at his bedside, comforting my dad with his presence as Dad prepared to make the journey from this life to the next. And I sang some more.

> When peace, like a river, attendeth my way,
> When sorrows like sea billows roll;
> Whatever my lot, Thou has taught me to say,
> It is well, it is well, with my soul.[1]

I was worshiping God in the very face of death. I was placing my mind's attention and my heart's affection squarely on Jesus Christ. The more I focused on him, the lighter my burden felt. And there in the room beside my dad, I took a posture of humility. I dropped to my knees beside his bed and continued singing the same old hymns that he had taught me as a little boy, the ones he would sing in his truck as we drove back and forth to work and to church and to my ball games with me snuggled up close to his side.

> Amazing grace! How sweet the sound
> That saved a wretch like me!
> I once was lost, but now I'm found;
> Was blind but now I see.

> When we've been there ten thousand years,
> Bright shining as the sun,
> We've no less days to sing God's praise
> Than when we'd first begun.[2]

For the first time in my life, I felt the hope of what I was singing. I sang those words hundreds of times growing up. But kneeling there beside my father's deathbed, I actually *believed* in the resurrection of the dead. I knew that death didn't have the final word, that Jesus was the prototype of a coming resurrection in a new world where God would make right all the wrongs that were ever done. I believed that my father would live again. I believed that my mother would live again. I imagined seeing my grandfather raised to life, my wife's grandfather, my grandmother . . . and suddenly I started laughing. For a second I thought I had snapped.

It was uncontrollable! I was overcome with joy. I knew that my family was still waiting for me out in the hallway and that they most likely assumed I was having a complete nervous breakdown from all the noise I was making. But I was so punchy I couldn't even get up off the floor. When I tried to stand up, I was laughing too hard to compose myself. My legs felt like tubes of Jell-O and my head was spinning with images of heaven.

I closed my eyes and imagined Jesus standing in the middle of a humongous crowd of people, thousands and thousands of people with their hands up in the air, shouting and laughing and dancing and calling out to Jesus. It was like a carnival and a parade mixed with a post–Super Bowl celebration. I imagined my mom there in the scene, like I had seen her in a picture right after she married my dad. She was wearing a yellow sundress and her eyes were closed as she roared with laughter at the sight of the celebration. Then I imagined my daddy, young and healthy and vibrant, making eye contact with me from across the mob of worshipers clamoring to see Jesus, and we smiled at each other. No words needed to be spoken. We understood.

Was this just a scene that I imagined? Or was it a vision of things to come, a prophetic view of a slice of the future that awaited me? Only God knows what heaven will be

Worshiping God beside my father's dead body . . . it was the weakest I'd ever felt and the strongest I'd ever been.

like for real, and while I don't know the details of the new heaven and new earth, the one thing I do know is this: I worshiped God that day on my knees beside that bed like

I had never worshiped him before. I lifted my hands to a God who is stronger than death. I raised my voice in praise to a God who can empty a tomb with a word. I fell on my knees beside the bed that held my father's lifeless body and saw a glimpse into a future where God would destroy death once and for all.

When I walked into that room I was swallowed by despair and regret. Gazing at my dad's motionless form was the hardest moment of my life. Yet, in a moment, the tide turned, the mood changed, the Spirit blew through the room, and I was aware that I was not alone. My earthly father had graduated to heaven but my heavenly Father was there with me on earth. Dad's life was in God's hands. His eternity was in God's hands. In an act of worship and surrender, I placed my life in God's hands once again, knowing that was the safest place my life could ever be. Worshiping God beside my father's dead body . . . it was the weakest I'd ever felt and the strongest I'd ever been.

From Position to Posture

It's not your *position* in life that makes you strong. It's your *posture* before God. When we embrace hard times and admit that we are powerless to change them, we leverage that weakness as it drives us to our knees before a powerful God who loves us and can help us. Tapping into his strength is what makes us stronger. Our strength has to be exhausted before we will reach for his in desperation. Getting low, humbling ourselves before God, is actually an act of worship. It's a posture of humility in the presence of God's great power that prepares us for the hard times we face in this life.

It's not about how *hard we work*. It's about how *well we worship*. Worship is ascribing worth to God. It's choosing to put ourselves in the proper place of humility and awe in response to the majesty and beauty of Christ. Worship is when we place our mind's attention and our heart's affection on who God is and what he has done. Or, as John the Baptist would say, worship is when we decrease and Jesus increases (see John 3:30). It's when we become smaller and he becomes bigger.

Worship is an awareness of God's presence, God's activity, and God's holiness. You don't have to be on your knees to worship God, but it's hard not to be mindful of how strong and kind he is when you're down on the ground in an uncomfortable position, knees pressed against the hard floor and heart contrite before the One who made you. That's a posture of submission. That's a place of real strength. You're never stronger than when you're on our knees, because that's what worship really is: placing all your attention and affection on God.

Worship and Weakness

The last thing we want to do when we're weak is to worship. Yet worship is the very thing we must do if we want to be stronger. Pain breaks us wide open, and something within our own depths cries out to the depth in God. It is interesting how often in Scripture we see a connection between pain and worship. For example, in Acts, Paul and Silas are imprisoned for preaching the gospel. But when they get to prison, as the specter of midnight hovers over them, they begin to sing to God—and it is their worship that

God ultimately uses to get them out of lockup. One minute they're singing, and the next minute the prison doors are knocked wide open by an earthquake. Worship can change a situation in a second!

Far from being some kind of random obligation, worship is much more akin to breathing. Worship opens up our hearts and minds to something outside and beyond ourselves. Pain has a way of constricting us, of making us feel imprisoned

Worship allows us to embrace the pain we're feeling while trusting the good that God is doing.

in our own heads. But as it was for Paul and Silas, worship has the power to break us out. It reminds us that the pain of the present is temporary, that we are part of the story of God, an eternal story in which death does not overcome. Worship allows us to embrace the pain we're feeling while trusting the good that God is doing.

No wonder, then, that in seasons of weakness there is something in us that longs for transcendence. We long for the "otherness" that worship gives us, the perspective it brings. And yet worship is not exactly an "escape" from our lives either. Worship grounds us in that which is real, in the tangible hope of God. We may still feel like we are on the bottom of the ocean, but worship allows us to tap into the goodness of God from the surface and breathe hope into our lungs like scuba divers breathe from their air tanks—even while all is still dark and uncertain.

The book of Revelation has so much human suffering—so many images of the people of God hurting, persecuted, losing their own lives. And yet one of the most overlooked themes of the book of Revelation is worship. Over and over again, we get magnificent scenes of worship—worship at the throne of God, worship from humans and angels and strange creatures—adoration of all forms lavished onto God. It should be no wonder that a book that so vividly illustrates the drama of human suffering is full of so much worship—the former necessitates the latter.

It is not just that we can worship when we're weak but that there is no other time in life when we can worship more purely. Not only can we worship in the midst of the trial, but the trial itself seems to draw the worship out of us. At first, it seemed counterintuitive for me to automatically give God praise and thanks while my family members were dying one after the other. But I chose to worship in my weakness. I chose to praise God alongside the panic, like the Old Testament character Job, who lost every single thing that mattered to him and made a decision to place his attention and affection on God as he confessed, "The LORD gave and the LORD has taken away; may the name of the LORD be praised" (Job 1:21).

Worship takes on many forms and postures—singing, meditating, reflecting, lifting our hands, laying on our faces in reverence, kneeling, standing, journaling, shouting, or crying. There are as many forms of worship as there are emotions, which is good because worship is deeply emotional. These bodily practices ground us in the reality of our own created bodies and the One who created them. Worship is what connects us with God—with life! True worship, then, does not require us to lose touch with our true feelings but to acknowledge and embrace them.

The relationship between worship and weakness is especially provocative in Psalms, the ancient prayer and worship book of the church. People who expect the psalms to be full of good cheer are often shocked once they really read them, as so many of the psalms are not songs of celebration but of lament with questions like *Where have you gone, God? Why have you abandoned me? Don't you see where I am and how much I hurt?* One of the most fascinating aspects of the psalms is that there is no clear demarcation from when the lament stops and the praise starts. The two move seamlessly in and out of each other, celebrating the goodness of God and speaking honestly about the pain of human experience in truly raw language.

There are whole psalms devoted solely to grieving and mourning, an aspect of communal worship that we often downplay to our peril in the Western church in particular. But often what we see in the psalms is a distinct pattern of people crying out to God, being ruthlessly candid with him about the depth of their brokenness, and then finally giving way to trust. A beautiful example of this is Psalm 142:

> I cry aloud to the LORD;
>> I lift up my voice to the LORD for mercy.
> I pour out before him my complaint;
>> before him I tell my trouble.
> When my spirit grows faint within me,
>> it is you who watch over my way.
> In the path where I walk
>> people have hidden a snare for me.
> Look and see, there is no one at my right hand;
>> no one is concerned for me.
> I have no refuge;
>> no one cares for my life. (vv. 1–4)

It is only after the psalmist has cried out to the Lord and let out all of the anguish and grief that the complaint can give way to trust. Thus the very next words are, "I cry to you, LORD; I say, 'You are my refuge, my portion in the land of the living'" (v. 5).

That is the way worship works. We cannot worship *around* our pain. We can only worship *in* and *through* our pain. It's through a primal, authentic expression of the inadequacy within us that we make way for trust. We cannot conceal any of it before God. When we make our sorrow available to God, we become open enough that real trust becomes possible. Opening up our confusion and depression before the Lord becomes a kind of invitation for him to work in and through them. It becomes an invitation to hope. Worship can create an oasis for us in dry, desert places. I had been depressed for years. Losing nine family members in twelve years took its toll on me. Yet the one thing that helped me transcend my circumstances, that alleviated the discouragement even if just for a moment, was taking my eyes off my situation and placing them on Jesus in private and corporate worship.

Worship and Submission

Worship is about surrender. It's an act of submitting our will, circumstances, and desires to God. We are required in worship to find a way to say yes to God from exactly where we are. So instead of languishing in our pain, we submit to whatever God may want to do in us through it, even if we don't know what the outcome will be. During the writing of this book, I was having coffee with my friend Jonathan, and we were fleshing out this idea of worship flowing out of weakness. He said that sometimes we have to hit the bottom in order to find a solid place to plant our feet. That new perspective resonated deeply within my soul.

There is no greater illustration of this in all of Scripture than in the life of Jesus himself, particularly his agonizing night in Gethsemane. It was the last night before the cross and the heartache was swallowing him whole. Anguish churned in his gut, thick and hot. The smell of his own sweat filled his nostrils; he could taste his stomach acid in the back of his throat. He dreaded the tearing that he would feel—in his muscles and skin to be sure, but that would not hurt nearly as much as the sense of being torn from his Father.

Everything in him screamed, *If there was any other way, any other way at all!* But in the supreme act of submission, he let even the depth of his anguish give way to trust. He knew his Father not only to be good but to be goodness itself, and that letting go even in this moment must be giving way to that goodness. Everything in him felt clenched, tense, tight. But as he finally exhaled again, the words rolled out of him in a resolved, decisive whisper. "Yet not as I will, but as you will" (Matt. 26:39).

Jesus agonized in the Garden of Gethsemane. Without pretense, he poured out his heart to his Father—all the grief, heartache, and longing. "If it is possible, may this cup be taken from me," Jesus prayed (v. 39). His ultimate fear was the same one I experienced these last few years—he feared separation from his Father. And yet we know that in that moment, Jesus had to say yes to the pain. He saw that the Father was going to do something extraordinarily redemptive through the suffering he was about to endure, so he didn't resist. He trusted in the goodness of his Father—so he submitted.

That is the supreme act of worship: to surrender our will into the hands of God, to stop striving, straining, pushing, and pulling. This whole matter is really about giving up the illusion of control.

We are not nearly as strong or as smart as we think we are, and until we admit that, our circumstances will have dominion over us. But when we own up to how small we are and place all of our hope and trust into God's capable hands,

---

This whole matter is really about
giving up the illusion of control.

---

we become strong in our weakness, because weakness leads us to worship and worship unleashes God's greatest power. Weakness is not, then, an *interruption* in the midst of your daily life. It is an *invitation* to worship God in the midst of your messed-up, out-of-control, unpredictable life.

Without crucifixion, there is no resurrection. Jesus's submission to his Father's will allowed him to embrace the pain of the cross. Surrender was what paved the way for the redemption of humanity. It is the most difficult thing in the world to say yes to God when he seems to be leading us straight through the middle of the valley of the shadow of death. But the truth of the psalms becomes especially resonant within us in such moments: "Weeping may linger for the night, but joy comes with the morning" (Ps. 30:5 NRSV). That is always true, no matter how much we struggle to believe it in the midst of trials and tests.

The death and resurrection of Jesus is the ultimate example of this. Jesus of Nazareth has overcome the grave, and worship is the way that we tether ourselves to him. That is why it is so important to make Jesus the object of our worship. As we worship him, we are conformed to his image. Worship makes us like the object of our worship. In the words of James K. A. Smith, "Human beings are at their core defined by what they worship rather than primarily by what they think, know, or believe. That is bound up with the central Augustinian claim that we are what we love."[3]

In a deep, experiential way, then, worship makes us what we love—it makes us like Jesus. And thus our own story is embedded more deeply in the story of Jesus's death and resurrection. Our own suffering is bound up in his suffering. But then the hope of resurrection infects us too. His resurrection is strong enough to swallow up all of our weakness. That's the reason I could fall on my knees, raise my hands, and lift my voice to God beside my father's deathbed—I knew he was very much alive and would one day be resurrected. As we worship, the story of Jesus—which really is the story of death and resurrection more than anything else—becomes our own story.

So remember that there was submission before crucifixion, and there was crucifixion before resurrection. To get to a place of resurrection, you must first embrace submission. It begins with giving up the illusion—the illusion of control.

GLORY

The Ability to Outlive Your Own Life

The glory of God is a living man; and the life of man consists in beholding God.

Irenaeus, *The Writings of Irenaeus*

Glory falls around us as we sob a dirge of desolation on the cross.

Maya Angelou, *Letter to My Daughter*

Is there a connection between weakness and the glory of God? Can hard times really reveal God's greatest power? Can they bring him glory? Absolutely. Jesus is seen in his greatest glory when the view is not obstructed by our own overinflated sense of pride and importance, and the most effective way for us to realize his sufficiency is when we are stripped down to utter weakness and forced to depend on his strength alone for all provision.

Tim Keller alludes to this paradox. In his masterful work *Walking with God through Pain and Suffering*, he writes, "Jesus Christ suffered, not so that we would never suffer but so that when we suffer we would be like Him. His suffering led to glory. And if you know that glory is coming, you can handle suffering too."[1]

C. S. Lewis described glory in two ways; he said that glory could be understood alternately as light and fame.[2] When a person or object exudes radiance, the light that emanates from them is their glory (the New Testament word is *doxa*, which means brilliance, beauty, or luminosity). Likewise, when a person or object is famous and well-known, they are said to have glory, such as the glory of the Roman Empire or the glory of the temple in Jerusalem. Glory, then, is understood in terms of radiance, brightness, fame, and magnificence. So how is God's glory revealed in our weakness? How is he made famous when we're filled with fear? How does his light shine brighter when our light seems to have burned out?

Seeing the Glory on My Father's Face

Fyodor Dostoyevsky once wrote, "The darker the night, the brighter the stars. The deeper the grief, the closer is God!"[3] I found his words to be poignantly true, especially as I watched my father journey toward death with grace and dignity with his eyes fixed on Jesus. I saw my dad exude the glory of God not once but twice, as he faced not just the fear of death but death itself. What I saw him do is what it means for God to be glorified in our hardest moments.

My dad's first open-heart surgery was, to put it lightly, an ordeal. After he had received numerous heart catheters and multiple stents, he was told his diabetes had blocked his arteries so badly that they had to be bypassed, but before they could perform surgery his blood pressure had to be stabilized. Then they had to thin his blood enough to operate, but not too much for fear that he would bleed to death. Finally, after six days in the cardiac ward, he was prepped for a triple bypass.

At 6:00 a.m., the surgeon entered the room with two nurses and the chaplain to check on my dad and take him back for anesthesia. He reminded my dad of what the procedure would be like; they would cut his chest open, remove his heart, repair and bypass the valves and arteries, place his heart back in his chest, reconnect everything, and shock the heart back into its natural rhythm, hoping it would respond. The surgeon said, "Mr. King, I will do my best to care for your heart the whole time it's in my hands."

Without hesitation, my dad spoke up. "Doc, I want you and your nurses to know something. Long before you planned to work on my heart, the Great Physician did surgery on me. He took my sinful heart and he performed a miracle by changing it and fixing it with his own blood that he shed for me on the cross. Over fifty years ago Jesus performed my first heart surgery, so when you hold my heart in your hands today, you won't be the first one. And if you've never let Jesus change your heart, you need to, because you will die one day from the sin in your heart. Jesus is the only one who can save you. If I die on that operating table, I know that I will be with the Lord. Can you say that you know that for sure?"

The nurses were bawling their eyes out. The chaplain was also crying. The doctor answered my dad and told him that he was indeed a believer bound for heaven. I was amazed, but I wasn't surprised. Dad had lived his life for the glory of God, trusting Jesus every step of the way. If he was going to die he wanted to shine the light on Jesus one last time before he stepped into eternity.

That's glory! In his weakest state and at the mercy of a team of doctors and nurses, he was pointing people to Jesus. He was telling them to look to Christ, to give their hearts to him and to consider where they would spend eternity when they died. The spotlight was on Jesus. He was illuminated. He was on display. God's glory was shining in that room through the weakness of a frail old man. My dad survived that surgery and was later released from the hospital, but we knew it was only a matter of time before the inevitable happened.

///////

Several years later the call that I had known would eventually happen came from his doctor. He informed me that Dad had experienced another heart attack during dialysis. This time there would be no procedure, no operation, no heart surgery. He was too far gone, too weak to undergo the trauma. They would cease dialysis treatments and keep him comfortable until the end. After a short conversation with my dad, my family and I made our way to the hospital, and eventually hospice, to spend the final few days with Joe King before his organs shut down and he slipped into eternity.

When we arrived in his room, it was already filled with a few friends and family members. Dad's brother and sister, my aunt and uncle, were there. My brother was there with his kids. Several cousins lined the walls. My father had given instructions to gather everyone at his bedside. The room was packed. He had some things to say before he died.

For years my dad had prayed for some of those people in that room to give their lives to Jesus. He had shared the gospel with them. He had witnessed to how Jesus had changed his life. He had reasoned with them and begged them to stop running from God. He knew it was almost time for him to go, so he leveraged what influence he had left, hoping they would not turn down a dying man's last request. It was his weakness that gave him the strength he needed for one final plea.

My family was the last to arrive. I couldn't believe how many people had crammed into that tiny space. I approached his bed and gave him a kiss. He embraced Sharie, then Jacob,

The only thing I want before I die is to know that the people I love the most have finally surrendered control to Jesus.

then Joseph, told us he loved us, and then he got down to business. If I live to be a hundred years old, I will never, ever forget what he said as he stretched out a trembling hand toward each person present.

"People, I'm going to die. Probably in the next few days. That's why I called you all here. Not so you could say your final goodbyes to me or cry all over yourselves. I brought you here so I could beg you one last time to stop running from God and give your lives to Jesus. I'm sick and tired of watching some of you ruin your lives when all you have to do is repent of your sin and ask Jesus to save you. Don't do it for me. Do it for you. Jesus changed my life over fifty years ago and he can change your lives tonight. The only thing I want before I die is to know that the people I love the most have finally surrendered control to Jesus."

You could have cut the air with a knife. Those of us who were Christians were torn between grief and joy, knowing he was dying but rejoicing in the hope of resurrection. The rest of the people in the room felt a mixture of conviction, awkwardness, and disbelief. How could a man on his deathbed be more concerned about them than he was about himself?

What we felt that night was heavy, thick, genuine glory. As a matter of fact, that is one of the words used to translate *glory* from Hebrew to English: *weight* (the Old Testament word is *kabod*, which means weightiness or heaviness). It's the fame of God, stronger than earthly kingdoms, more durable than the reigns of princes and presidents. It is the light of God, penetrating the darkest places and the hardest hearts, outshining the kingdoms and empires of men that have risen only to fall into the ash heap of history. In that tiny hospital room, we were all directed toward the risen Christ in his majesty, beauty, and grace. A dying man invited us to gaze on the Son of God and savor the sight of One both splendid and humble, One who would offer mercy and forgiveness to the most heinous offender and the most unlikely sinner. My dad outlived his own life, because God is still being glorified long after his life ended.

The famous American historical icon Jonathan Edwards, in his work *The Miscellanies*, alluded to the fact that God is glorified not only by his glory being seen and noticed but also by us rejoicing in it. That's precisely what happened that day. Our minds' attention and our hearts' affection had been turned to Jesus. He was made more famous. He was illuminated even more brightly by the trembling hand of a weary saint trying to point the way for those who were lost. I stood spellbound in a heavy cloud of glory, because the Holy Spirit himself was in that room. And I am still rejoicing in that glory.

The Glory on Stephen's Face

It was the glory of God on display in a hospital room that turned hard hearts toward Jesus, and it was the glory of God on a martyr's face that turned a self-righteous murderer into the greatest evangelist the world has ever known. As the stones began pelting faster and faster, not just ripping flesh but breaking his bones, Stephen could feel the lights start to go out. Moments before, he had been a man breathing fire against a tyrannical council, speaking words of truth heavier and more jagged than the rocks that were being thrown at him. He knew the council would make an example of anyone who would dare speak against them. He knew they dealt harshly with those they could frame as traitors to their religious tradition. He knew that to speak the hot words that swelled inside of him would be to incur their wrath. But he could not help but speak.

His own reputation was the farthest thing from his mind. Stephen's heart was captured by the terrible fidelity of Jesus's own love toward him. He had to speak. He saw through the Sanhedrin's display of false piety, their tactics of fear and violence to control his native people. Though they claimed to be people of the law, followers of the God whose admonition against murder was chiseled into stone tablets, they oozed murderous intent. They did not take kindly to prophets. There was a long line of dead bodies that bore witness to their corporate disdain of truth-tellers. He was not ignorant of what it would mean to speak truth to them.

But the words came like hot lava, and they kept on coming. Stephen had no agenda to make a name for himself. He had not come to play the martyr or the hero. He was not looking to become a legend. He was not looking to have his face chiseled in stone like an image in the Roman pantheon. It was only the beautiful, tender face of Jesus himself that Stephen saw as the rocks bounced off his skull. He knew that his Master's own face had been terrorized by the same forces of violence. With eyes full of blood, he kept looking up toward that face. Through cloudy eyes, Stephen saw the heavens open. *He saw the glory of God*. With a broken jaw now hanging loose, he spoke again. "Look . . . I see heaven open and the Son of Man standing at the right hand of God!" (Acts 7:56).

Already carried to sea by the hatred in their own hearts, the men covered their ears and shouted just before they picked up the last few stones that would splatter Stephen all over the ground. But he could not hear them. Jesus, the one who sits at the right hand of the Father in his proper place of honor, was not sitting anymore. The one who sits as a sign of kingly rule on the throne that reigns sovereign over all creation was on his feet. *God himself gave him a standing ovation. Jesus stood to welcome Stephen home.* The crowd was taunting Stephen. But he had seen glory. He was not distracted. In the face of death, Stephen just kept staring into the face that gave life and radiated glory.

As his own life gave way, he remembered the words that came across those beautiful lips when his Master's time came on Golgotha: "Father, forgive them, for they do not know what they are doing" (Luke 23:34). Feeling his lungs expand with air one last time, he mustered the breath to mirror what Jesus himself had said as he died only months ago. "Lord, do not hold this sin against them" (Acts 7:59). Then Stephen died, seeing the glory of God through the face of Jesus himself.

The one who sits as a sign of kingly rule on the throne that reigns sovereign over all creation was on his feet. God himself gave him a standing ovation. Jesus stood to welcome Stephen home.

The men who killed him saw the glory of God on Stephen's own battered face. That glory was hot, it was heavy, and it burned an indelible mark on Saul's soul as he watched Stephen die. Stephen's strength in his weakest moment revealed God's greatest power, a power that would soon stop Saul dead in his tracks and save him from his sin, change his name to Paul, and use him to change the world. Stephen outlived his own life. The glory is alive right now on this page.

The Glory Continues

It is this paradox that makes the gospel so strange and yet so true—that our darkest moments carry with them the weight of glory. That God makes himself known not *despite* the wreckage of our lives but *through* the wreckage itself. That even death can be a witness to the goodness of Jesus. The stoning of Stephen would seem to be one of the darkest moments in the early church, but from the horror of that moment, life came barreling through. While Stephen saw the face of Jesus, it was the face of Stephen in death that Paul would never forget. It was tattooed on his soul.

Later, it would be unbearable at times for Paul to live with the guilt. He had to remind himself over and over not to let himself dwell on the shame of his own violent past but to join Stephen in fixing his gaze on the face of Christ. He had to press on through the guilt and keep talking about Jesus, just like Stephen did. But through that horrible moment, the glory of God Stephen saw firsthand continued as Saul came to faith and became Paul. That same glory continued through Paul as he wrote his letters, and still continues as those letters are read across the world by millions of people every day. As a result of the weakness and death of a young man named Stephen, the dark heart of one man would come into light. And this man would in turn write over half of the New Testament and be known as one of the most revolutionary figures in world history. The glory of God was in Stephen's sermon. But the glory was much greater in Stephen's death—that's what God used to change the world.

Jesus prayed for his Father to forgive those who crucified him. Stephen prayed for God to fogive those who stoned him. And at the end of his life, Paul would pray for God to forgive those who abandoned him.

> At my first defense, no one came to my support, but everyone deserted me. May it not be held against them. But the Lord stood at my side and *gave me strength*, so that through me

the message might be fully proclaimed and all the Gentiles might hear it. And I was delivered from the lion's mouth. (2 Tim. 4:16–17, emphasis added)

All three of these men are showing you how to be stronger. Jesus. Stephen. Paul. There's no greater strength than to forgive your enemies in your weakest moment. And when you feel deserted and alone, the Lord will stand at your side and give you strength.

How might God use your weakness? In what ways will he showcase his power through your pain? You can't predict what God will do, but you can dream, you can imagine, and you can submit whatever hard times you're facing to a God who is able to bring beauty from ashes. The day is coming when the glory of God will be witnessed in its full form for

---

There's no greater strength than to forgive your enemies in your weakest moment.

---

all creation to see. The day is coming when graveyards will be emptied and the resurrection life of Jesus will overcome the power of death in its full splendor. On the cross, love triumphed over death. And it is only a matter of time until that triumph is played all the way out. The glory of God will be realized when God's kingdom comes to earth and there is no longer any barrier between earth and heaven. Revelation 21 gives us this beautiful picture of that which is yet to come:

> I saw the Holy City, the new Jerusalem, coming down out of heaven from God, prepared as a bride beautifully dressed for her husband. And I heard a loud voice from the

throne saying, "Look! God's dwelling place is now among the people, and he will dwell with them. They will be his people, and God himself will be with them and be their God. 'He will wipe every tear from their eyes. There will be no more death' or mourning or crying or pain, for the old order of things has passed away." He who was seated on the throne said, "I am making everything new!" Then he said, "Write this down, for these words are trustworthy and true." (vv. 2–5)

This is the hope that gives your own weakness a sense of scale and perspective in light of the world that is coming in Christ: a day in which there will be no more death, mourning, crying, or pain. A day in which God himself will personally wipe away your tears. A day in which all things will become new. The future glory of God is what gives you the strength to endure when you cannot see that glory now. When there is nothing anyone can say or do to make the hurt go away or the confusion subside—that glory holds you up. If death does not have the final word over you, and the glory of God is going to one day overrule all of your weakness, then no pain is final. No wound will go unhealed. The glory of God is coming, and I can't wait.

But in the meantime, God gives us glimpses of his glory even now. Even now, we get a taste of the love that triumphs over death. We still feel our weakness. And we see his strength. We may not feel as strong, or be as strong, as we would like to be. Our strength is not perfect, but it doesn't have to be—only his strength is perfect, and it is made perfect in our weakness. In our own weakness, in our brokenness, fear, and confusion, the life and the glory of God are surging through us into the world. The resurrection power of Jesus is at work within us, even when we feel like we are wasting away. He is with us and in us and for us, and by his grace . . . *we are getting stronger.*

> Therefore we do not lose heart. Though outwardly we are wasting away, yet inwardly we are being renewed day by day. For our light and momentary troubles are achieving for us *an eternal glory that far outweighs them all.* So we fix our eyes not on what is seen, but on what is unseen, since what is seen is temporary, but what is unseen is eternal. (2 Cor. 4:16–18, emphasis added)

EPILOGUE

In many ways, my dad thought of himself as a simple man. He never attempted to travel the world and preach the way I do. He wasn't concerned about living his life out in front of the world—he just lived his own story as fully as he knew how. But I think his story is a story worth telling.

There have been moments when the pain of losing my parents (and numerous other relatives) in these last few years, with all the other scars I've picked up as I age and face hard realities of life, has felt like too much for me. But the glory of God I saw at work in my dad's life continues to pick me up and carry me through the darkest moments. And it is my hope and prayer that the same glory so present in my dad's death reaches all the way to you now, wherever and however you are reading this, and that even now you can begin to see something of the glory of God at work in your own weak and broken places.

Two years before my father's death, I wrote him a letter on Father's Day. I wrote it as a way to commemorate his life and his legacy while he was still alive, but it seems like the best way to pay tribute to him one more time here. The glory in and on my dad's life was strong. I hope that something of the strength God gave him by his Spirit will be real for and in you now.

Daddy,

Where do I even start? I guess I will start by saying the first two things that come to mind.

Thank you, and I love you.

You are, without a doubt and without equal, the greatest man I have ever known. I cannot think of a single man of any age or background who can compare to you. You have been everything as a daddy that a son could ever want or need. You were kind and loving to me, providing for my basic needs as well as giving me gifts that were extravagant, like the go-cart that I nearly killed myself on and the Ford Bronco that I flipped on that dirt road.

You made me work and I am so glad you did, because now I love work and cherish the memories of you and I working together on the farm, or wiring the new house, or working on the tractor. If I had known what special times those were while we were working together, I would have paid closer attention.

Thank you for teaching me to tell the truth, to respect my elders, and to love the church. These lessons are now bearing fruit in my life as I become a man. I see a cynical world that loves lies, but you always valued honesty and the truth above all things. Thank you for disciplining me when I lied and for not giving in when I begged you to let things slide. You saw into the future and knew that one day I would have to live in a world that was tough, where people have to be accountable, and you forced me to learn things the hard way. Thanks for making me go to church and sit still during preaching. I am so blessed that you were my Sunday school teacher when I was young. To see my daddy standing with a Bible every Sunday morning instructing me and all my buddies in the ways of Christ went way deeper into my soul than I realized then, but I am realizing it now.

Thank you for being faithful to your wife. You came home every night after work. You helped around the house, made sure the bills were paid, and loved her faithfully, even though times were very hard and there were many struggles. I know how to love my wife now because you showed me how for all those years. How does a young man even know how to be married or how to love his wife without the kind of example I had in you?

Thank you for adopting me. I cringe at the thought of how my life would have turned out if God had not put me in your home. You rescued me and took me as your own, as indeed I am, and even as I type these words, I weep at the very thought that my life and ministry exist because you took me in and loved me.

Thank you for teaching me to pray, to tithe and give, to work hard and take pride in my accomplishments, to save my money and put God first in my finances, and to be compassionate to everyone, especially those in need. You were a man of God when I was just a little boy. Now I am becoming a man of God because of you, and I am raising my boys to be men of God because I want them to have the character and integrity that you have. I want them to be like you, Daddy, because you are such a great man.

Thank you for being there. You were always home if you weren't at work. You took me fishing. You came to all of my ball games. You called my name from the stands on Friday nights and even at my college graduation. You played baseball with me in the front yard. You took us to the mountains and to the beach and to Washington, DC. You worked so hard all those years to give us a good life, and you were there. You were the constant presence in my life that I needed so badly then, and still need now.

I am so sorry that you have been so sick these last years. I know it has been more difficult than I could ever dream, but even as you laid on the hospital bed, about to be taken back for triple bypass, you grabbed the doctor and the chaplain by the hand, and told all the nurses that you loved Jesus and that he would take care of you, and you took five minutes in a room full of medical professionals to share your testimony of how God had been your faithful friend and father since you were ten years old. That one five-minute testimony before open-heart surgery made the biggest impression on me. At sixty-seven years old, you have more influence on me now than you ever have.

Thank you for fighting to stay alive. You could have given up and gone to be with Jesus years ago, but your love for your wife, your boys, and your grandchildren made you stay here and fight for your life. I want you to keep fighting because I want my boys to know you. They need to know the greatest man I have ever known, and I just pray that God will give you more years with us.

Finally, on this Father's Day, I want you to know how much I still need you. I cannot imagine a world without Joe King. I always think about you and feel loved, secure, safe, and cared for. You are the one I call for counsel, advice, wisdom, and encouragement. The thought of not being able to see you or pick up the phone and hear your voice makes me afraid. What would I do without you? Who would I be without you? You chose to be a daddy to me even though your daddy left when you were a boy. Somehow, by God's grace, you were everything I ever needed. You were perfect. The perfect daddy. My best friend and my hero, and I love you more today than I ever have.

Happy Father's Day from your biggest fan.

Big C

ACKNOWLEDGMENTS

The primary acknowledgment must go to adversity. Though it's a difficult concept to personify, without adversity there would be no experience through which God could have worked so effectively and efficiently to show me the things I've seen or to change me in the ways that I've been transformed. So thank you, adversity, for your relentless pursuit of pain in my life and the perspective you've given me on everything that's really important.

To my lovely wife, Sharie—you're the most precious and perfect gift I've ever received besides my salvation. You've walked with me through thick and thin and have been my true best friend.

To Jacob Thomas and Joseph Austin, my little bitty boys, for bringing me so much joy and making my dreams of being a daddy come true.

To my staff at CKM/Crossroads: Justin and Jess, Zach and Ashley, Gillis and Colin, Jordan, Brian, and Erin—we really are just getting started.

To my band of brothers: Brian Burgess, Perry Noble, Jonathan Martin, Jordan Hibbard, Steven Furtick, JD Greear, Todd Gaston, Dean Parker, Carl Cartee, Justin Brock, Steve Haimbaugh, David Lancaster, Tracy Jessup, Eric Pratt, Justin Kintzel, Ian McIntyre, Johnnie Moore, Bruce Frank, Derwin Gray, Christian Newsome, Chris Conlee, Shawn Smith, Jon Doster, Paul Marshall, Will Merritt, Chad Speck, David Nasser, and Keith Hibbard.

To my pastors and mentors: Wilkes Skinner, Jake Thornhill, Billy Graham, David Chadwick, Ray Hardee, Evans Whitaker, Ronnie Powell, Todd Still, Robert Canoy, and Jimmy Epting.

To NewSpring Church—thanks for being a place where it's ok not to be ok, but it's not ok to stay that way.

To my old friends Eddie, Matt, Grant, Stuart, Wil, Lee, Seth, Trey, Loring, Chunks, Larry, Todd, Dwayne, Jeff, Chris, and David.

To my mother, Jane, and my brother, Brad; to Uncle Bill and Uncle Dan, and my cousins.

And to my father, Joe . . .

NOTES

Introduction

1. Tim Keller, *Walking with God through Pain and Suffering* (New York: Penguin, 2013), 8.

Chapter 1 Brokenness

1. Henri Nouwen, *Can You Drink the Cup?* (Notre Dame: Ava Maria Press, 2006), 87.

Chapter 2 Humility

1. C. S. Lewis, *Mere Christianity* (London: MacMillan, 1952), 92.

2. As quoted in Joseph Demakis, *The Ultimate Book of Quotations* (Raleigh, NC: LuLu Enterprises, 2012), 253.

3. As quoted in John M. Mulder, *Finding God: A Treasury of Conversion Stories* (Grand Rapids: Eerdmans, 2012), 121.

Chapter 3 Testimony

1. Cormac McCarthy, *All the Pretty Horses* (New York: Alfred A. Knopf, 1992), 135.

2. Jonathan Martin, *Prototype* (Carol Stream, IL: Tyndale Momentum, 2013), 64.

3. Eric Liddell, "Victory over Circumstances," *Knowing and Doing*, Summer 2012, http://www.cslewisinstitute.org/webfm_send/1387.

4. Pamela Cushing, "Jean Vanier on Becoming Human," *Jean Vanier: Becoming Human*, accessed December 29, 2014, http://www.jean-vanier.org/en/his_message/jean_vanier_on_becoming_human.

5. Henri Nouwen, *Out of Solitude*, rev. ed. (Notre Dame: Ava Maria Press, 2004), 38.

6. Ibid., 34.

Chapter 4 Presence

1. As quoted in Josiah Bull, *Letters of John Newton* (Carlisle, PA: Banner of Truth, 2007), 26.

Chapter 5 Strength

1. John Stott, *The Cross of Christ* (Downers Grove, IL: InterVarsity, 2006), 78–79.

Chapter 6 Regret

1. As quoted in Charles R. Swindoll, *Paul: A Man of Grit and Grace* (Nashville: Thomas Nelson, 2002), 22.

Chapter 7 Vulnerability

1. G. K. Chesterton, "Christmas," *All Things Considered*, Project Gutenberg ebook, March 7, 2004, http://www.gutenberg.org/files/11505/11505-h/11505-h.htm#CHRISTMAS.

2. For more information on Brene Brown, visit YouTube.com and search for her TEDTalks, such as "Brene Brown: The Power of Vulnerability," YouTube video, 20:49, uploaded January 3, 2011, by TED, https://www.youtube.com/watch?v=iCvmsMzlF7o.

3. Brene Brown, *The Gifts of Imperfection: Let Go of Who You Think You're Supposed to Be and Embrace Who You Are* (Center City, MN: Hazelden, 2010), 6.

Chapter 8 Understanding

1. As quoted in Gregory Privitera, *Research Methods for the Behavioral Sciences* (Thousand Oaks, CA: SAGE Publications, 2013), 469.

2. Jerry L. Sittser, *A Grace Disguised: How the Soul Grows through Loss*, exp. ed. (Grand Rapids: Zondervan, 2004), 79.

3. C. S. Lewis, *The Problem of Pain* (New York: HarperCollins, 1996), 91.

4. As quoted in Ray Glennon, "July 27th to August 2nd: Drinking the Cup," *Nouwen Book Discussions*, July 26, 2014, http://wp.henrinouwen.org/rgroup_blog/?p=518.

5. C. S. Lewis, *A Grief Observed* (London: Faber and Faber, 1961), 48.

Chapter 9 Worship

1. "It Is Well with My Soul," words by Horatio G. Spafford, music by Philip Bliss (1873).

2. "Amazing Grace," words by John Newton (1779), music by James P. Carrell and David S. Clayton (1831).

3. James K. A. Smith, interview by David Neff, "You Can't Think Your Way to God," *Christianity Today*, May 24, 2013, http://www.christianitytoday.com/ct/2013/may/you-cant-think-your-way-to-god.html?paging=off.

Chapter 10 Glory

1. Keller, *Walking with God through Pain and Suffering*, 181.

2. C. S. Lewis, *The Weight of Glory: And Other Addresses* (New York: Harper-Collins, 2001).

3. Fyodor Dostoyevsky, *Crime and Punishment* (Kiddy Monster Publication, 2013) Google Play ebook, loc. 513.

Clayton King was born in 1972 to a fifteen-year-old mother who chose adoption over abortion. He converted to faith in Christ at age fourteen and began speaking in prisons, churches, and public school assemblies. Modeling his ministry after his hero Billy Graham, he began traveling internationally in high school and has been in thirty-eight countries and forty-five states. Clayton has spoken to nearly four million people since 1987 and is the founder of Crossroads Summer Camps and Crossroads Missions. He is also the president of Clayton King Ministries, a 501-c-3 nonprofit ministry and humanitarian organization. Clayton is a distinguished professor of evangelism at Anderson University, a teaching pastor at NewSpring Church, and the author of twelve books. He ministers and writes with his wife, Sharie, and they also homeschool their two amazingly cute sons, Jacob and Joseph. He loves black coffee, good books, the woods, and the mountains.

For more information, visit www.claytonking.com.

MISSISSIPPI COLLEGE

A Christian University

FAITH ▪ FAMILY ▪ FUTURE

EXPERIENCE WHAT
HIGHER LEARNING
IS ALL ABOUT

As a member of our MC family, you will be offered a wide variety of activities to keep you busy, challenging academics to keep you sharp, and a spiritual foundation to keep you grounded. Our smaller size gives you bigger opportunities for your career, for friendships, and for personal growth. Join our growing family. We have a place for you here.

FIND OUT MORE ABOUT ALL THE POSSIBILITIES AT MC!
www.mc.edu/stronger

admissions@mc.edu | 800-738-1236 | Clinton, MS 39058

BE BOLD

PURSUE YOUR PASSION.
PROCLAIM CHRIST.

When choosing a college, I knew I wanted a place that would not only guide me in refining my craft but also guide me into a deeper recognition of God's truth. Cedarville compels life direction by nurturing life purpose.

Madison Hart '16

LEARN MORE:
cedarville.edu/stronger

CEDARVILLE
UNIVERSITY.
for the **WORD OF GOD** and the **TESTIMONY** of **JESUS CHRIST**

ClaytonKing
MINISTRIES

CKM

EVENTS · MISSIONS · MENTORING · SPEAKERS
PREACH THE GOSPEL & MAKE DISCIPLES

SPEAKERS

Clayton King Ministries is committed to serving the Body of Christ by providing biblical teachers who can connect with teenagers, college students, and adults. Check out our website to invite a speaker to your next event!

MENTORING

We offer personalized trainings in short-term and long-term capacities. Clayton King's Coaching Network provides specific ministry training sessions throughout the year, and our Crossroads Discipleship Home is a yearlong discipleship and internship program for young adults. Consider joining today!

WWW.**CLAYTONKING**.COM

GO
AND MAKE
disciples
OF ALL
NATIONS

go | CROSSROADS MISSIONS

#gowithCR

WWW.GOWITHCR.COM

CROSSROADS Summer Camp

"Crossroads Summer Camp will be the best week of your summer!"
—Clayton King

In 1996 Clayton King started Crossroads Summer Camp to provide a unique camp experience for students and leaders. At Crossroads you'll be refreshed by the message of the gospel, participate in amazing activities, worship with hundreds of other students, and be encouraged by the most relational staff in the country.

Anderson University—Anderson, SC

WWW.CROSSROADSSUMMERCAMP.COM